The Life and Times of
BABA RAMDEV

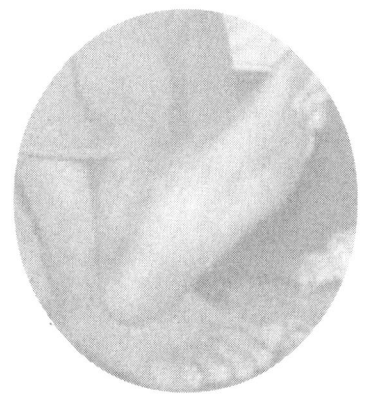

By the same author

HERO *Volume 1*
THE SILENT ERA TO
DILIP KUMAR

HERO *Volume 2*
AMITABH BACHCHAN TO
THE KHANS & BEYOND

The Life and Times of
BABA RAMDEV

Ashok Raj

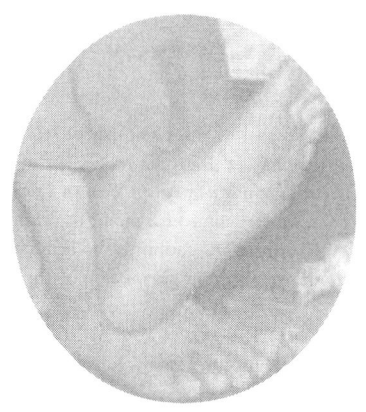

HAY HOUSE INDIA
Australia • Canada • Hong Kong • India
South Africa • United Kingdom • United States

Hay House Publishers (India) Pvt. Ltd.
Muskaan Complex, Plot No. 3, B-2 Vasant Kunj, New Delhi-110 070, India
Hay House Inc., PO Box 5100, Carlsbad, CA 92018-5100, USA
Hay House UK, Ltd., 292-B Kensal Rd., London W10 5BE, UK
Hay House Australia Pty Ltd., 18/36 Ralph St., Alexandria NSW 2015, Australia
Hay House SA (Pty) Ltd., PO Box 990, Witkoppen 2068, South Africa
Hay House Publishing, Ltd., 17/F, One Hysan Ave., Causeway Bay, Hong Kong
Raincoast, 9050 Shaughnessy St., Vancouver, BC V6P 6E5, Canada

Email: contact@hayhouse.co.in
www.hayhouse.co.in

Copyright © Ashok Raj 2010

First published 2010

The moral right of the author has been asserted.

All rights reserved. No part of this book may be reproduced by any mechanical, photographic, or electronic process, or in the form of a phonographic recording; nor may it be stored in a retrieval system, transmitted or otherwise be copied for public or private use – other than for "fair use" as brief quotations embodied in articles and reviews, without prior written permission of the publisher.

Cover painting : Priya Kuriyan
Designed and typeset at
Hay House India

ISBN 978-93-80480-16-9

Printed and bound at
Thomson Press (India) Ltd.

In fond memory of my parents

Mrs Sushila Devi
&
Mr B. R. Hoogan

*Where there is yoga,
there is prosperity.*

Baba Ramdev

Contents

Preface	9
Introduction	13
Chapter 1 Maharishi Patanjali, Guru Gorakhnath and Ancient Yoga Traditions	19
Chapter 2 Ramdev's Predecessors	49
Chapter 3 Ramdev's Path of Self-Discovery and Yoga-Healing Philosophy	77
Chapter 4 Establishing Medical Efficacy of Yoga	115
Chapter 5 Ramdev's Mass-Awakening Doctrine	145
Chapter 6 Agenda for Global Rejuvenation	191
Chapter 7 Ramdev's Indigenous Hero's Ascent and the Fault Lines	201
Glossary	219
Index	227

Preface

When my nephew, Kaushal, gifted me a CD on Ramdev's yoga way back in 2002, the seer had just entered public life. I did not take him and his yoga seriously at that time as I have always been very sceptical about the Godmen and preachers holding a sway on the huge religious gatherings and TV channels. As a scientist, I have also been least bothered about the matters of God and the divine scheme of things. I thought he was yet another guru of the yore in the making, seeking the attention of gullible masses. But as he started stirring up people with his yoga and the way he began articulating the social concerns of our times with so much gusto and conviction, I soon became curious about this man in saffron.

Like his teeming followers, I soon found him very forthright and down to earth, empowered with a vision that was both very refreshing and mind boggling. I realized that this sanyasi had, at least, captured and articulated the ills of the Indian society and the world at large, despite his spiritual-Hindu affiliations. And what is more, he denounces religious dogmas and obscurantist views and presents yoga as a pure secular practice for health, and self- and social-empowerment. He, in fact, has emerged as a powerful propeller for creating a morally strong, caring civil society that common man always dreams about.

 Preface

I thus found this people's indigenous hero of our times a fascinating and yet intriguing subject for study. I, therefore, decided to study the yoga and mass-awakening doctrine as being propounded by him that could help in locating this doctrine in the past spiritual traditions as well as in the critical milieu of our times. But the problems were many. Foremost was the spread of this demagogue's philosophical and ideological tenets over innumerable discourses and writings characterized by much repetition and verbose. Also, there were no serious academic studies that could inform me in developing a theoretical framework of my work. Therefore, it became pertinent for me to identify his ideas on spiritual and social life from the vast repertoire of his sayings and speeches, and present them as a unified comprehensive work on this avid thinker and crusader.

No words can be enough to convey the debt of gratitude that I owe to Ganesh Khetriwal of Patna for generously throwing open his entire personal collection of Baba Ramdev's photographs for use in this book. His contribution to this volume is of immense value.

I express my deep gratitude to Ashok Chopra of Hay House for choosing the manuscript for publication, virtually instantaneously and for offering me his immense guidance for restructuring the work so as to enhance its appeal and contemporary relevance. I convey my deep thanks to Raghav Khattar, Padma Pegu and Aeshna Roy of Hay House for lending a very valuable scholarly and editorial expertise for this work.

I must thank my sister, Aruna Mahendru, a keen follower of Ramdev, for assisting me in keeping a track of the rapid progress the seer has made in the development of his ideas and actions for the past ten years. I also thank my colleague,

 Preface

Rakesh Kapoor, for his invariable comments on the draft of this work and offering me highly useful reference material.

I also thank my colleagues and friends – Surendra Prakash (a spiritual master in his own right), Shradha and Ravi Kashyap, Manju, Sankalp and S. K. Sharma, Rumjhum and Girish Kumar (and their sons, Charu Kartikeya and Kirti Vinayak), Tanvi and Ankit, and Professor Pradeep Biswas – for their immense support for this work.

Thanks also to the library staff of the Nehru Memorial Museum & Library, New Delhi; Jawaharlal Nehru University; the Sahitya Akademi; and the Centre for the Study of Developing Societies, New Delhi.

No author can escape acknowledging the love and care bestowed on him by his wife in difficult and anarchic times of writing a book. To Madhu, I present this work for her extremely worthy support and enforcing on me a strict writing schedule to honour the deadlines. And what to say about our impatient son, Pallav – he kept pestering – 'Oh daddy! When will I be able to impress my teachers and friends by showing-off this book of yours?'

Ashok Raj

Introduction

In today's world, the perpetual sickness of the human mind and body, and the disparate search for true happiness and a genuine feel of *sukkha* have become the most wishful longing for all of us. The growing deteriorations in the very quality of life have intensified a quest for a better way of life through a world view that could become a viable alternative to the dominant materialistic milieu which determines how we perceive the world and ourselves. This quest is focused on rediscovering and reinstating the lost ancient wisdoms and a host of alternative ideas and practices from the treasures of traditional knowledge – which, it is argued, could inspire the making of 'happy individuals and happy society'.

Amidst the frantic ideological and spiritual movements currently spearheaded the world over by some of the best thinkers and practitioners towards setting a spiritual-ecological-equitable-integral agenda for global society, there has arrived, rather all of a sudden, a curious man from nowhere. Baba Ramdev has emerged as the new ideologue of the global spiritual-consciousness movement, seeking to link it with the ideals of the current ecological and anti-materialistic campaigns. With his own version of holistic yoga as his ploy for instituting the universal right to health, he wants to unleash an euphoria

 Introduction

of human resurgence to cure the world of its maladies and install a caring and morally vibrant civil society all around. For this, the seer has proposed two distinct ideological alternatives to the current established order of the world – pranayama (breathing exercise) and the yogic way of life as the key to health restoration and well-being; and manifestation of an enabling spiritual environment for personal and social transformation.

Ramdev's arrival once again underlines the continuing significance of Oriental spiritualism the world over as it offers perhaps the most promising insights for the creation of a 'new spiritually awakened man' – a man at ease with himself and with the world around him. As is well known, the Indian spiritual traditions have thrown up highly revered masters in the past – Sri Aurobindo, Swami Vivekananda, Swami Dayananda, Lahiri Mahashaya, Paramhansa Yogananda, J. N. Krishnamurty, Raman Rishi, Swami Sivananda, Swami Shivananda Sarasvati, Shri Yogendra, Meher Baba and Osho, among others. Several new thinkers also arrived on the scene to heal the wounds of a suffering humanity. They include the yoga legends B. K. S. Iyengar, K. Pattabhi Jois, Bhagwan Nityananda, Swami Satyananda Saraswati, Swami Niranjanananda and Sri Sri Ravi Shankar.

Ramdev has gained mass adulation in a short span of time. As the propeller of an indigenous mass health movement, this celebrated man of our times has caught the public imagination perhaps as vividly as, say, Mahatma Gandhi, Swami Dayananda, Ramakrishna Paramhansa and Swami Vivekananda did in the last century. As his yoga discourses have become a national passion, he has acquired a mass following that only a few other celebrities have had in independent India. Despite sporadic criticism, Ramdev continues to gain ascendancy as the new

 Introduction

indigenous national hero. The spectre of his popularity is, indeed, comparable with that of our icons in some other fields – Bismillah Khan, M. S. Subbalakshmi, K. L. Saigal, Dilip Kumar, Lata Mangeshkar, Amitabh Bachchan and Sachin Tendulkar, among others.

Ramdev, with his unique package of pranayamas, claims to cure virtually all diseases including even the deadly ones like cancer and AIDS. The seer has adopted a two-pronged strategy to bring in people within his healing domain. First, he asks them to introspect their lifestyle in the context of today's wild consumerism, and second, using the 'neighbourhood sport club' model for his yoga camps, he inspires them to shake off their lingering lethargy to rejuvenate themselves both physically and mentally through his brand of yoga. With his quick, virtually off-the-cuff, assuring solutions for innumerable health problems, the master has created his own niche in the health-care domain of the country. He has also initiated among his followers a process of self-discovery geared towards a wider cultural and spiritual self-confidence and assertion.

Ramdev's highly inspiring discourses also represent the first-ever mass mobilization built around a highly effective use of modern media technologies to establish and sustain the outreach of his messages. In his orange robes and jet-black, long flowing hair and beard, and with his lean physique and oodles of energy, this ever-smiling, unassuming talker with an earthy sense of humour shows not a single streak of the arrogance of an intellectual or a thinker. He reminds us of those jovial, friendly teachers in school who with their sheer spontaneity and zeal would create an intimate rapport with their students.

Surprisingly, Ramdev seems to have created a space for appreciation not only among the laity but also among the

Introduction

country's intellectual class, corporate think-tanks, scientists and doctors, and even some radicals having allegiance with the country's Left. Sri Sri Ravi Shankar, his world-renowned contemporary, says, 'If an individual can be credited with reviving yoga in this country, it is solely Swami Ramdev. He has spread yoga to such an extent that sooner or later, one has to embrace it.'

Yet, Ramdev is not merely a healer of the individual. This saffron-clad yoga revolutionary seems to have set for himself a higher purpose. With his package of yoga and holistic living as his ploy, he wants people to undergo a process of self-discovery and contemplation to build a collective cultural consciousness and nationalist feelings, and become proactive partners in the processes of national reconstruction.

The seer's holistic doctrine reflects, adherently or inadvertently, significant ideological influence of several past spiritual masters and social reformers, the foremost being Swami Vivekananda, Swami Dayananda Sarasvati, Sri Aurobindo, Swami Sahajanand Sarasvati and Mahatma Gandhi. Though the seer appears to be lacking the profound philosophical depth of these thinkers, he has imbibed and articulated some of their basic tenets in his discourses. In this way, his work represents a valuable synthesis of the ideas and actions of his predecessors' great minds.

However, despite Ramdev's emergence as the new ideologue of a national and global spiritual resurgence, he is still to find a place in academic discussions. This work is an attempt to fill the gap. It is a study on the making of the Ramdev spectacle with all its phenomenal success, mass enthusiasm and adulation, and controversies. It seeks to locate his philosophy in today's socio-cultural milieu, while tracing its origins in Indian spiritual history, and the past landmark

 Introduction

reformist movements that have been initiated in the country by earlier path-breakers. This work also examines the building of the seer's transnational image as the new-age world guru seeking to install with all his romantic and upbeat fervour an agenda for global rejuvenation.

Chapter 1

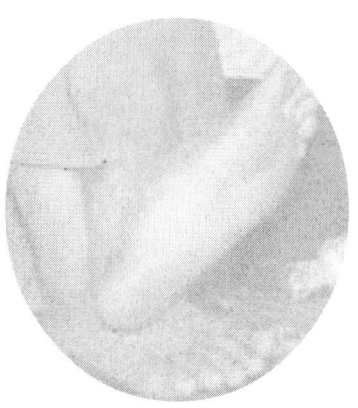

Maharishi Patanjali, Guru Gorakhnath and Ancient Yoga Traditions

Just as the naturally pure crystal assumes shapes and colours of objects placed near it, so the Yogi's mind, with its totally weakened modifications, becomes clear and balanced and attains the state devoid of differentiation between knower, knowable and knowledge. This culmination of meditation is Samadhi.

Ancient Indian philosophy was built around three main streams. The Sankhya philosophy provides an exposition of maya, the delusion of the world. The Vedanta teaches the eternal nature of the cosmos and its reality; yet, it states that philosophy alone cannot bestow the certainty that is born of experience. It is Yoga that teaches the way out of delusion: how to walk firmly, without stumbling, in the raging waters of maya, in full command of one's life and inwardly singing with joy. The Yoga teachings set forth are not mere pious maxims but the principles and practical guidelines to live a better, more fulfilled life, both outwardly and inwardly. They also pronounce the need for everyone to practise them.

Indian yoga with all its antiquity is believed to have been invented by the Primeval Man, Adinath, another name for God Shiva. In the Vedic tradition, it is the ancient philosopher, Maharishi Patanjali, who laid the foundation of Yoga as it is known today. In his classical work, Yoga-Sutras,[1] the sage codified into a text of brilliant compression the fundamental principles and practice regimen of Yoga.

Patanjali, a disciple of the famous grammarian, Panini, was a great philosopher, grammarian and physician, all rolled into one. His other two important works are Mahabhasya, a commentary on grammar, and Ayurveda, the celebrated treatise on the ancient Indian system of medicine. The evidence that the author of the Yoga-Sutras was also this genius is found in the commentary of the Caraka-samhita, written by Cakrapani (AD 1060). In his introductory sloka, he mentions the introductory verse of Raja Bhoja's commentary (not later than AD 1055) on the Yoga-Sutras that Patanjali composed the works on grammar, yoga and Ayurveda. Also, Helaraja, a celebrated scholar of his times, in his commentary on the Vakyapadiya (seventh century AD), states that the author of this work attributes the three treatises on medicine, grammar and yoga to the same Patanjali.[2] However, Dr S. Radhakrishnan, the author of *Indian Philosophy*, is of the opinion that the author of the Yoga-Sutras is not later than AD 300 and possibly Sage Patanjali flourished in the second century BC.[3]

In its essence, Patanjali's Yoga doctrine as laid down in Yoga-Sutras is in tune with the two other pillars of Indian philosophy, Sankhya and Vedanta, which were evolved to inspire man to realize the Self, and through this realization to reach out to the Absolute Truth about the world. According to Sankhya, whatsoever is obtainable through the senses is delusive and of no use, and the source of all life's pain, uncertainty and suffering essentially is this very delusion. Therefore, by cleansing one's mind and controlling one's thought processes, one should banish delusion from the consciousness and seek an understanding of the higher inner reality. Yoga sets up the very process of this understanding whereby, through complete willingness and discipline, one is able to depollute one's mind and achieve control over one's body and thought processes. Finally, the seeker reaches the state of equanimity in which he is able to perceive the world in its true light and to accept that truth in its entirety. Thus, he realizes the oneness between the Self and the Absolute Truth.

This way, Yoga, indeed, is the culmination of human wisdom cultivated through a deep understanding of physiology, psychology, ethics and spirituality.

The Yoga-Sutras

Yoga-Sutras[4] sought to prepare the ground for an inner exploration of the Self, and therefore the higher Absolute Truth, through the practice of Ashtanga Yoga, the eight yogic stages prescribed for a seeker. This work, in fact, marked the beginning of a spiritual resurgence in response to the distortions that were being inflicted on Hindu religion – firstly, by the complex ritualistic practices in the form of massively organized fire sacrifices to please the Gods; and secondly, by the misinterpretations of the sculptures by the vested priestly class as a way to dislodge genuine seekers in search of true spiritual solace.

Yoga-Sutras is divided into four sections (*pada*s) titled Samadhi Pada (profound or abstract meditation), Sadhana Pada (means of accomplishment), Vibhuti Pada (psychic faculty) and Kaivalya Pada (final state of released soul). It consists of 196 aphorisms, or sutras (literally meaning 'threads') – the long series of interlinked ideas are weaved together to form the grand wreath of an overriding philosophy. The compositional beauty of Yoga-Sutras is so terse and precise that nothing significant has been added to the text in the last 2,500 years.

Patanjali heralds his Yoga-Sutras with a one-line definition of yoga – 'Yoga is the cessation of movements in consciousness.' He then builds his discourse taking up the core philosophical issues step by step, elaborating on understanding of the mind, the body, their interaction, and the consciousness. This is followed by a rendering of the path for self-realization and the physical and intellectual benefits of practising yoga, warning along the way about the possible pitfalls, saying that years of accomplishment can be destroyed by a few moments of unaware indulgence. Significantly, nowhere in the text does he talk about renunciation, use of self-torture, penances, or deprivation for one's emancipation, but rather exhorts to live life fully in abundance and bliss.

Samadhi Pada

In the first chapter, the Samadhi Pada, Patanjali deals with the aims and forms of yoga, and the different methods of attaining yoga. It starts with the definition of yoga as *citta-vrtti-nirodha* (suppression of mental functions). This *pada* is an exposition on the ways the mind can be worked upon to overcome its natural worldly urges. According to the sage, the *vritti*s (functions) can be either *klista* (painful) arising from *klesha*, which are opposed to *viveka* or discriminatory knowledge. The *vritti* can be suppressed either by *abhyasa* (practice) or by *vairagya* (spirit of detachment and indifference to worldly desires or passions).

The sage then presents an elucidation of the supreme consciousness and the various stages of samadhis (a self-absorbed, detached state of being) through which one could enter into the highest level of spiritual awareness. The impending mental distractions are discussed along with the ways to conquer them – cultivating attitudes of friendliness towards all, compassion for the unhappy, delight in the virtuous, disregard towards the wicked, reaching the state of undisturbed calmness through either controlled exhalation or retention of the breath, and concentration on subtle sense-perception or on the supreme, the ever blissful light within. Patanjali says:

Just as the naturally pure crystal assumes shapes and colours of objects placed near it, so the Yogi's mind, with its totally weakened modifications, becomes clear and balanced and attains the state devoid of differentiation between knower, knowable and knowledge. This culmination of meditation is Samadhi. (Samadhi Pada: Sutras 33–41)

In samadhi, the yogi finally gains *ritambhara prajna*, the true wisdom, drawn solely from the awareness of the Absolute. He is now in a state of complete detachment from all the four spheres of gross materiality (*annamaya kosha*), physicality (*pranamaya kosha*), psychology (*manomaya kosha*) and intellect (*vijnanamaya kosha*). He is not only beyond the world but beyond himself as well, his consciousness merely remaining attached with the purely spiritual sphere of the *anandamaya kosha*. The sage calls this stage the Nirbija Samadhi, in which all seeds of earthly impressions are erased from the yogi's consciousness.

According to Patanjali, samadhi is of two kinds – *samprajnata* (state of bliss in which the meditator has the knowledge of his object of meditation) and *asamprajnata* (in this state, the distinction between knower, knowledge and which is to be known absolutely disappears). *Isvara*, or super-consciousness, is described as the One who is unaffected by *klesha* (discussed in second chapter), *karma-vipaka* (fruit of action) and *asaya* (latent impressions).

The sage also elaborates on the factors that cause distraction of mind (*citta-viksepa*) and work as hindrance to yoga. These are: *vyadhi* (disease), *styana* (incapability of mind), *samsaya* (doubt), *pramada* (absence of thought about the means of samadhi), *alasya* (laziness or languor), *avirati* (hankering for objects of sense), *bhrantidarsana* (false knowledge), *alabdhabhumikatva* (non-acquisition of the object of samadhi) and *anavasthitatva* (non-fixation of the mind on the acquired object of samadhi). The distraction of mind leads to *dukkha* (suffering), *daurmanasya* (mental depression), *angame-jayatva* (shaking of limbs), *svasa* (in-breathing) and *prasvasa* (out-breathing). The distraction of mind can be overcome by developing *maitri* (friendliness), *karuna* (compassion), *mudita* (joy at others' happiness) and *upeksa* (equanimity or indifference) towards fellow creatures. A happy mind is endowed with *punya*. The mind is pleased also by *pracchardana* (emitting the inner wind through the nostrils) and pranayama.

Sadhana Pada

Composed in 55 sutras, the Sadhana Pada, the second chapter, further stresses the need for absolute control over the *chitta vritti*s (thought processes) to attain the highest union or yoga. It asks the yogi not to be a passive 'spectator', but a pro-activist to gain mastery over the Divine Spectacle. *Pramana*s, or the means of valid knowledge, are three — *pratyaksa* (perception), *anumana* (inference) and *agama* (sacred scripture, the Vedas). To reach the final goal, it recommends *viveka-khyati*, or discriminatory knowledge, as the means necessary to have a true understanding of the Path. It deliberates on ignorance as the major hindrance for reaching the state of supreme consciousness.

The maharishi now discusses the five *kleshas* or sources of suffering — *avidya* (nescience), *asmita* (egotism), *raga* (attachment), *dvesa* (hatred or enmity) and *abhinivesa* (instinctive clinging to worldly life and physical enjoyments, and fear of death). One can get rid of impurities by practising the *yogangas*, the eight steps or methods of achieving knowledge of the Self – *yama* (restraint), *niyama* (observance of ethical rules), *yogasana* (posture), pranayama (breath control), *pratyahara* (withdrawal of the sense from sense-objects and other distractions of the outside world), *dharana* (deep devotion or abstraction), *dhyana* (meditation on an object, a place, or a subject) and samadhi (concentration, absorption; the ultimate stage of yoga meditation). Patanjali terms the collation of these eight steps as Ashtanga Yoga.

The sage then prescribes the practice of karma and Ashtanga Yoga as a practical means to overcome ignorance and other *klesha*s for acquiring this union. He further describes the different kinds of thought formations and practices to control them, and the different kinds of samadhis culminating in the highest experience of Nirbija Samadhi. Patanjali says:

> As the impurities get destroyed due to the practice of the accessories of yoga, there arises the illumination of knowledge. (Sadhana Pada: Sutra 28)

The Ashtanga Yoga or Raja Yoga (the 'royal path'), indeed, is the central edifice of Patanjali's Yoga system and constitutes one of the *shad-darsana*s or classical systems of Indian philosophy. It is presented as a comprehensive meditative method for mind control by channelling mental and physical energies into composite spiritual improvement of the practitioner. It inspires the fullest development and control of any one of the human faculties – the mind, emotions, life force, or the physical body. Such partial perfection is then allowed to spill over to one's entire being.

Vibhuti Pada

The term '*vibhuti*' means manifestation or residue. In this chapter, the sage delineates all the accomplishments – the siddhis, or the powers – that come as the result of regular yoga practices. He opens his discourse with *dharana*, which he defines as fixing the mind on a particular *desa* or region (*desabandha*). This is followed by the definitions of *dhyana* and samadhi. The above three together, as the final three limbs of Ashtanga Yoga, lead to what the sage calls *samyama*, the ultimate perfection manifesting as *citta-nirodha*, concentration and calm. *Samyama* gives rise to *viveka-jnana* or discriminatory knowledge, the sine qua non of liberation. These practices for a yogi lead to acquiring *kayasampat* (wealth of the body), which consists of beauty, grace, strength and an adamantine body.

The author further prescribes *indriyajaya* (control of the senses), by dint of which the yogi acquires speed like that of the mind (*manojavitva*). Proper performance of yoga manifests as *sarva-jnatrtva* (omniscience) and *vairagya* (detachment, indifference), finally resulting in the destruction of the very seeds of the faults and paves the way to *kaivalya*, the highest goal of yoga.

The maharishi now elaborates on the subtle states of awareness and the advanced techniques of practising *samyama* and various manifestations of siddhis that follow. The sage says:

> The yogi, who has only the knowledge of the distinction of *Sathva* and *Purusa*, acquires mastery over all things and omniscience. (Vibhuti Pada: Sutra 50)

Kaivalya Pada

Patanjali defines *kaivalya* as the state of absolute detachment attained through the destruction of all qualities devoid of *purusartha* or the power of *citta* (consciousness) which is established in itself (*svarupa-pratistha*). The 34 sutras of this last (fourth) chapter of the Yoga-Sutras elaborate on the siddhis, which are achieved by the application of (particular) mantras, *tapas* (austerities, penance) or samadhi. A yogi who attains *kaivalya* becomes an entity who has gained independence from all bondages and achieved the absolute true consciousness or *rtambhara prajna*. The sage says:

> The complete extinction of the qualities, devoid of action for the *Purusa* is *Kaivalya* or (it is) the power of consciousness which is established in its own form. (Kaivalya Pada: Sutra 34)

At the end of this chapter, he discusses samadhi that occurs before the final stage of *kaivalya* is reached and when a kind of samadhi called Dharmamegha arises. It is when a yogi, after acquiring *viveka-jnana*, is absolutely free from attachment or hankering and becomes a holder of true understanding and knowledge.

The basic doctrine of the Yoga-Sutras, therefore, is that the individual soul (*jiva*) is real, eternal and pure. It is, however, involved in the world of sense-objects, and seeks evanescent ends. The ultimate goal of *kaivalya* is a state in which the soul remains isolated in its own form, and is free from *prakriti* and from the bondage of birth and death. *Jivanmukti* (liberation when alive), not *videhamukti* (liberation in a disembodied state or death), is the ideal of Yoga.

Guru Gorakhnath: The Proponent of Hatha Yoga

Centuries after Patanjali, Guru Gorakhnath, the eleventh-century founder of the avant-garde Natha Yogi cult, pioneered the doctrine of Hatha Yoga through a brilliant exposition of Patanjali's Ashtanga Yoga in his celebrated work, Goraksa-Sataka.[5] Gorakhnath was the disciple of Guru Matsyendranath, who inspired the founding of several avant-garde religious cults in the following centuries. These cults were to counter the casteist and ritualistic undercurrents of Brahmanism as seen in the later doctrines of Kabir, Ravidas and Guru Nanak, among others.

Gorakhnath, the yogi, was a living legend with a large following in many parts of the subcontinent. Over the centuries, his cult had continued to appeal to the hearts of the people. Even today, his followers are found in parts of Uttar Pradesh, Punjab, Sindh in Pakistan, Gujarat, Bihar, Bengal and Nepal. They are variously known as yogi, Gorakhnathi and *darsana*, and generally have the appellation of Natha (the master). The female followers are called Nathni. They adore big earrings and, therefore, also have the appellation of *kanphata* (split-eared). In western India, they are known as Dharmanathi (or Dharamnathi) after Dharamanath, a noted disciple of Gorakhnath.

Scholars differ on the place of Gorakhnath's origin and the time he belonged to. George Western Briggs in his classic work[6] concludes that he hailed originally from East Bengal. Nepal and Punjab are also said to be among the places of his origin. Marathi saint Jnanesvara's reference to Gorakhnath in his famous work (AD 1290) on the Bhagavad Gita is perhaps the solitary dependable evidence about the date of this yogi.[7]

The Natha cult took the form of a distinct school called Natha Samprodaya, largely on the lines of Buddha's Sangha. The catholicity of this school included in its ambit not only Hindus and Buddhists, but also Muslims.[8] The Natha Samprodaya churned out a vast volume of literature around the legacy of Gorakhnath, both in Sanskrit and vernaculars, particularly in Punjab and Bengal. In Bengal, Natha literature took shape in two renderings, one focusing on Gorakhnath's persona and the other on Natha philosophy and worship (as seen in Gopichand's Maynamati-govinda), both expressed in numerous ballads and *sakhis* (rhymes).

One significant development that exemplifies the grand secular character of Natha school was the intellectual and spiritual role of several Muslim yogis in enriching the Natha doctrine and building its popular appeal. These yogis contributed a considerable amount of Natha literature in Bengali. Notable among them were Ali Raja (eighteenth century AD), commonly known as Wahed, Kanu or Kanu Fakir, the author of Jnana-sagara; Syed Sultan (seventeenth century AD), the author of Jnana-pradipa and Jnana-cautisa; Muhammad Safi, who penned Nur-Kandila; and Murshid, who wrote three treatises – Vara-masya, Yoga-kalandar and Satya-jnana-pradipa. These works represented a very significant edifice of a composite spiritual culture through a powerful blending of Nathism and Sufism, prevailing in the society at that time. The Islamic yogic literature of Bengal, in fact, is a product of this syncretism. Besides the popular stories of Gorakhnath and Gopichand, Muslim yogis also created a vast repository of popular songs stressing the hollowness and baneful effects of worldly pleasures, and emphasizing the importance of yoga as indispensable for overcoming decay and death, and attaining liberation. The Muslim blend of yoga was also pursued in other parts of India.

 The Life and Times of Baba Ramdev

For instance, the Bhartharis of Uttar Pradesh are Muslims who appear to have descended from their yogi ancestors.

Goraksa-Sataka

In his Hatha Yoga doctrine, Gorakhnath propounded the idea of attaining spiritual perfection, the perfect physical form (poise, balance and strength), and balanced mind and body through the severe practice of controlling mind and body. The postures or movements – the asanas, pranayama and mudras – are called *kriyas*, which are contemplative in nature and were originally intuited by yogis during meditation. A practitioner purifies his mind and body through the practice of observances and resistance towards passions, and through control over the respiratory process by these *kriyas* to improve the body's physical health and clear the mind in preparation for meditation in the pursuit of enlightenment. As he reaches the stage of deep meditation, all blockages (diseases) in the causal, subtle and physical bodies get removed. The Hatha Yoga doctrine was also elaborated by Guru Meenanath, Guru Chouranginath, Raja Bhartuhari and Raja Gopichand.

Gorakhnath authored a series of 15 treatises but the Goraksa-Sataka, also known as Jnana-Sataka, is his most important, and the basic work. The Hindi version is Goraksa-Paddhati.

Gorakhnath begins the rendering of the Goraksa-Sataka with the remark that it is a work on Hatha Yoga. He offers salutation to Guru Matsyendranath and exhorts the reader to practise yoga, which is the fruit of the wish-yielding tree in the shape of *sruti*, and which puts an end to the misery of the world (*bhavatapasya samanam*). He then enumerates six *yogangas*.

The sage states 84,00,000 asanas as having been described by Lord Siva, and 84 selected by Him for practices. From these, he selects and describes only two – Siddhasana and Padmasana. He then elaborates on the physiology of the human body in the spiritual framework. According to him, the body is a house of one column with nine doors, presided over by five tutelary deities, and contains six *cakra*s, sixteen *adhara*s, three lakh *nadi*s (arteries) and five sheaths. He also explains their locations in the body.

Among the *nadi*s, the author says, 72 are prominent and the ten principal ones are Ida, Pingala, Susumna, Gandhari, Hastijihva, Pusa, Yasasvini, Alambusa, Kuhu and Samkhini. They terminate in the following parts of the body, respectively: left nostril, right nostril, hole in skull, left eye, right eye, right ear, left ear, mouth, male organ and anus. He then elaborates on the working of the vital forces through *nadi*s, which, as he says, originate in the *kanda* (base) and have their ends in the openings of the body. The first three – Ida, Pingala and Susumna – are the most important as they are the conductors of the *pranavayu*, or the paths of life force. They are of critical importance in pranayama and in raising the kundalini shakti.

The author now enumerates the following *adhara*s: *padangustha* (big toe), *mula* (anus), *guda* (rectum), *medhra* (penis), *uddiyana* (above navel), *nabhi* (navel), *hrdaya* (heart), *kantha* (throat), *ghantika* (soft palate), *jihvamula* (root of tongue), *urdhva-danta-mula* (root of upper front teeth), *nasagra* (nose tip), *bhrumadhya* (in between eyebrows), *lalata* (forehead) and *brahmarandhra* (top of head).

Gorakhnath moves on to discuss six principal *cakra*s and their respective locations within the body: Muladhara (at the base of the spinal cord), Svadhisthana (at the root of the penis or the penis itself), Manipuraka (in the navel region), Anahata (in the heart), Visuddha (in the throat) and Ajna (between eyebrows, within the cranium). The location and function of ten winds within the body are also described. *Prana, apana, samana, udana* and *vyana* are hailed as the principal vital powers. This elucidation is followed by the descriptions and effects of five mudras – Mahamudra, Nabhas, Uddiyana, Jalandhara and Mula. He finally heaves praises on pranayama and meditation.

The seer discusses the main goals of Hatha Yoga: control of mind and body; retention of breath; retention of semen; experiencing rapturous feelings resulting from the union of *rajas* (kundalini) and *bindu* (Siva) at different levels in the body; and ultimate release. The means prescribed are purification by pranayama, asanas, mudras and *bandha*s.

The ultimate destination of kundalini, which is supposed to penetrate the above-mentioned six *cakra*s, is the Brahmasthana, the place of final bliss (Brahmananda) where kundalini is united with Siva in the *sahasrara* (thousand-petalled lotus). Thus, the ultimate aim of the Natha yogi's Hatha Yoga is *jivanmukti* (liberation while alive) as hailed by Patanjali. Gorakhnath says:

> O excellent men! Practice (Hatha) Yoga, the fruit of the-tree-of-wishes, the sacred word whose branches (yoga schools) are frequented by birds (Brahmans and seekers), which brings to an end the misery of the world. (Goraksa-Sataka: Sutra 6)

Swami Swatamarama and Hatha-yoga-pradipika

The virtues of Hatha Yoga and its practice were further elaborated by Swami Swatamarama, a disciple of Gorakhnath, in his work Hatha-yoga-pradipika.[9] In this brilliant exposition, the yogi describes in detail all the asanas, pranayamas, mudras and *bandha*s. This work is essentially a manual for scientifically taking one's body through stages of control to a point where finally the yogi realizes his well-being and imbibes the virtues of *viveka-jnana*. The sage says:

> Hatha-vidya is the temple of shelter to those who are afflicted by endless sorrow. Hatha-vidya is the supporting tortoise to the innumerable people engaged in yoga. (Upadesa I: Sutra 10)

The Hatha-yoga-pradipika is divided into four chapters, called *upadesa*s. The author opens his work by extolling Guru Matsyendranath and Guru Gorakhnath as the ones who knew the *hatha-yoga-vidya*, and by whose grace he knew it as well. In the opening verse, he hails the *hatha-yoga-vidya* as a stepping stone to the sublime Raja Yoga. Later in the text, he again lauds this yoga: 'There is no world without Raja Yoga, no night without Raja Yoga, even varied Mudras are of no use without Raja Yoga, and nobody really knows the actual greatness of Raja Yoga.' He further writes that only this yoga brings the integration of the mind, that is, culminates in a state where the subject–object duality disappears. He lays down Hatha Yoga and Laya Yoga as the means to the attainment of Raja Yoga, and says Raja Yoga and Hatha Yoga are complementary to each other, and one is not possible without the other.

Sage Swatamarama now lays down a set of pre-conditions for the aspirant of Hatha Yoga. He should live in a *matha*, situated in a kingdom with a pious king, where alms are easily available and which is free from disturbances. In this dwelling, he should live within the space of one *dhanus* (i.e., four cubits). The *matha*'s architecture should consist of one small door, without window, level and holes, not too high, too low, or too long; it should be clean and well-smeared with cow dung; and it should be free from insects. Enclosed by a surrounding wall, it should have a *mandapa* (hall in front), a raised seat and a well.

The author further stresses the importance of the guru (guide, mentor or preceptor) for a neophyte. The aspirant should practise *brahmacarya* and eat good food in moderate quantity, with one-fourth of the stomach left unfilled. In no case the yogi should become *alpahara* (having insufficient food); otherwise, increased gastric fire will quickly consume the body. A list of articles of food to be consumed are specified: wheat, rice, barley, grains that ripen within 60 days (swastika or pure grains), milk, ghee, sugar candy, butter, sugar, honey, dry ginger, vegetable patola (loofah), fruits, the five kinds of pot-herbs (called *jivanti, vastumulya, aksi, meghanada* and *punarnara*) and *mudga* (a kind of kidney bean). A yogi, therefore, should eat foodstuff that is nourishing, very sweet, mixed with oil or ghee, nutritious for the elements of the body, pleasant and of proper quantity. A large variety of food is prohibited for a yogi: bitter, sour, pungent, salty food and cooked but cold food that is heated again, dry food (devoid of ghee or butter), food of bad taste, sour gruel, sesamum oil, mustard, wine, fish, meat of goats, curd, buttermilk, horse gram, jujube fruit, oil cake, asafoetida, garlic, *sake* (an edible leaf, generally fried) and *saltpetre* (rock salt).

The sage also prohibits a yogi from warming oneself with fire (in winter), enjoyment of women, visiting holy places, fasting, mortification of the body and company of bad people. The aspirant should also be constantly aware of the six lapses that are stated to spoil yoga: overeating, over-exertion, talkativeness, *niyamagraha* (i.e., adoption of wrong habits, which include morning bath with cold water, fasting by night, subsisting on fruits alone), association of people, and greediness. On the other hand, the six qualities that foster yoga are: zeal or energy, courage, patience, true knowledge, *niscaya* and abjuration of bad company.

The author hails asanas as the first accessory of Hatha Yoga which leads to *sthairya* (firmness of body and steadiness of mind), freedom from disease and lightness of the body. According to him, asanas are 84 in number, but he describes only the following four essential ones: Siddhasana, Padmasana, Simhasana and Bhadrasana (also called Goraksasana). He delineates the other 11 asanas and their effects – Svastikasana, Gomukhasana, Virasana, Kurmasana, Kukkutasana, Uttanakurma-asana, Dhanusasana, Matsyendra, Pascimatana, Mayurasana and Savasana.

The sage then sets out to elaborate the sequence of Hatha Yoga practices – asana, followed by various kinds of *kumbhaka*s and mudras, and concentration on *nada* (described later). The first chapter concludes with observations about the benefits reaped from siddhi. According to him, practice of yoga leads one to siddhi, be he a young man, old or very old, diseased or weak. Significantly, the author stresses that mere study of the scriptures or assuming a yogi's dress or talk about yoga do not lead to siddhi – only conforming action in the prescribed manner does.

The second chapter deals with the practice of pranayama, which, he cautions, should be undertaken only under the guidance of the guru. The author mentions the diseases caused by wrong yogic practices, and prescribes their cures by yogic methods. In the end, he delineates the persona of a yogi who has perfected Hatha Yoga – slimness of body, brightness of face, capacity for hearing *nada*, very clear eyes, freedom from disease, control over the seminal fluid, stimulation of digestive fire and complete purification of the *nadis* (arteries).

The third chapter is focused on Kundalini Yoga. Kundalini, the energy string, is the potential form of prana, or life force, lying concealed in the human body and activated through spiritual practice. It is in the form of a coiled-up serpent (literally, kundalini in Sanskrit is 'coiled up') at the base of the spine. When roused, it pierces all the *cakras* and the *granthis* (knots), through *nadis* or channels, up the psychic channel of the *sushumna* (empty path), which runs from the base of the spine to the brain. When this kundalini energy, in the first *cakra* at the root of the spine (Muladhara Cakra), is raised up through the rest of the *cakras* until it reaches the seventh and the highest *cakra* (Sahasrara) located at the crown of the head, self-realization occurs. This induces the blissful state of samadhi. Kundalini can be awakened by practising the following mudras and bandhas: Mahamudra, Mahabandha, Mahavedha, Khecari, Sambhavi Mudra, Uddiyana, Mulabandha, Jalandhara-bandha, Viparitakarani, Vajroli and Sakticalana.

Among the mudras, Mahamudra can lead to overcoming of all kinds of sufferings and even death. The master of this mudra gets rid of consumption, leprosy, constipation, abdominal diseases and indigestion, and keeps off wrinkles, grey hair and shaking due to old age. It helps the mind reach the centre (*kendra*) in the mystic centre between the eyebrows. Sambhavi Mudra leads to concentration on the internal spot in any *cakra* from Muladhara upwards. Interestingly, the author illustrates the distinction between the knowledge of scriptures and the attainment of Sambhavi Mudra by comparing common courtesans who are available to all and a housewife (*kulavadhu*).

Khecari Mudra (also described in the third chapter), when practised until the yogi experiences *yoga-nidra*, leads to *turya* (fourth state of consciousness) beyond *jagrat* or working, *svapna* or sleep, and *susupti* or profound slumber. The Khecari Mudra saves him from poison, disease and even death, and keeps off old age. He does not suffer from excessive sleep, hunger and thirst. His intellect is not clouded. When he seals the cavity in the upper part of the palate, he experiences no emission of seminal fluid even if embraced by a young and passionate woman.

Among the bandhas, Uddiyana Bandha helps its master overcome suffering and death, too, and makes an old man look young. With Mulabandha, the quantity of urine and excrement gets reduced. Jalandhara-bandha destroys all maladies of the throat. Viparitakarani Bandha increases the gastric fire and removes wrinkles and grey hair. Its daily practice should be performed to whet appetite. Its daily practising also helps to overcome suffering, and if performed for one *yama* (three hours), one can conquer death. Vajroli leads to a pleasant smell of the body, while Sahajoli, if included in Vajroli, gives divine sight to the yogi. Sakticalana makes one free from diseases and helps in acquiring the siddhis.

The fourth chapter is devoted to samadhi, which confers supreme bliss. The following synonyms of samadhi are given in the text: *rajayoga*, *amaratva* (immortality), *laya* (absorption), *tattva* (truth), *sunyasunya* (void, yet not void), *parampada* (supreme state), *amanaska* (mindless, i.e., transcending the mind), *advaita* (non-duality), *niralamba* (supportless), *niranjana* (devoid of impurities), *turya* (fourth state of consciousness), *jivanmukti* (liberation while alive) and *sahaja* (unforced intuitive natural state). The author describes samadhi as merging of the mind in the self, in much the same way as salt gets dissolved in water. In this state, *jivaiman* (individual soul) is united with supreme soul. He gives the essential prerequisites of reaching this state as the compassion of the genuine guru, renunciation of sexual pleasures, and awakening of the kundalini.

The author now enumerates the working of the mind in relation to prana. The two are mingled like milk and water. Mind is fickle like mercury, and when it is active, it makes the prana also active. But when the mind is stilled, prana is suspended. Mind becomes immobile when absorbed in *brahmarandhra* by means of *kumbhaka* – just like mercury is solidified by the use of herbs. Prana, thus, becomes stable, and there is stability of semen, which leads to stability of body. Thus, an indescribable bliss is experienced. *Laya* (absorption) occurs when breathing is suspended. The comprehension of objects and senses ceases because no longer can the previously acquired impressions and tendencies (*vasanas*) now occur. The yogi should be able to stop prana flow through the Sun (or Pingala *nadi*) during day and through the Moon (or Ida *nadi*) during night, making it flow through Susumna alone.

For meditation, the author suggests that the yogi should place the Self (*atman*) in the midst of *akasa* (Brahman), and the *akasa* in the midst of the Self. When he reduces everything to the presence of the eternal *akasa*, and thinks of nothing else, he enters the state that is like void within–void without. This void is like a pot in space (*akasa*); full within–full without or full, like a pot in the ocean with infinite water around. Since the entire universe is the fabrication of thought only and the mental activities are created by thought alone, one can acquire perfect repose by transcending the mind. When the mind is dissolved in contact with the Absolute Reality, like salt in water, the state of absoluteness (*kaivalya*) is reached.

The author now dwells on devotion to *nada* (*anahada* or the unstruck eternal sound) as taught by his teacher Gorakhnath. This practice, he says, is suitable even for those who are devoid of learning and are unable to comprehend the Truth directly. After entering into Mukta-asana and Sambhavi Mudra, the practitioner should listen, with concentrated mind, to the inner sound through the right ear, which finally is clearly audible in the pure Susumna passage. Samadhi, when reached through contemplation on *nada*, brings in ample bliss that is unparalleled and beyond any description. As Brahmagranthi is pierced by pranayama, there arises the bliss from the void (*sunya* or *akasa* of the heart). Then, various tinkling sounds (like those of ornaments) and finally the *anahada dhvani* is heard in the middle of the body. The yogi in this state acquires a lustrous and exquisitely fragrant body, free from diseases, and has a heart full of life force and bliss.

The author finally extols the attainment of *unmani* state within a short time, which, he says, is suitable even to people of mediocre intellect for the attainment of Raja Yoga. In this condition, the body becomes motionless like a log of wood, and the yogi does not hear even the sound of a conch or a drum.

The Natha Yoga as seen in Goraksa-Sataka and Hatha-yoga-pradipika differed in many ways from other schools of Yoga which regarded the complete severance of the body and the dissolution of the spirit as the essential prerequisite of liberation. The Natha yogis believed in the attainment of liberation with a body transmuted by the fire of yoga. The yogi, possessed of such a spiritually empowered body, gets relieved of *asuddha maya* (principles of defilement) and acquires *visuddha maya*, which enables such a body to act as a purified, dynamic entity.

The Natha literature also reveals a large Buddhist influence. For the Nathas, the holy places of pilgrimage are located within the body, and described under the categories of Pitha, Upapitha, Ksetra, Upaksetra and Sandotha, which are similar to the Buddhist practice. The Buddhist idea of *sahaja-sunya*, or the state of nirvana, as the ultimate aim of a seeker is also found in Natha literature. One significant reading of this work is its proclamation that worship of the Gods is not more than a secondary means to reach out to the Higher Being or the self-realized and blissful Self.[10] Thus, Hatha Yoga philosophy, since its inception, has remained spiritually unique as it transcends the boundaries of any one religion or cult.

The Vyasa-Bhasya

This work, written in the fourth century AD, is a standard commentary on Patanjali's Yoga-Sutras, penned by Veda Vyasa, a yogic sage, different from his namesake, the legendary author of the epic, Mahabharata. The text is flushed with several quotations attributed to sage Pancasikha, a renowned scholar of Sankhya philosophy.

Vyasa-Bhasya elaborates the postulates of the original text and proclaims that one's own direct experience is the only ultimate source of knowledge; all other *pramanas* (evidence) are dependent on it. It advocates the unqualified equality of rights of both men and women in spiritual matters. It teaches friendliness not only to the human beings, but also to all creatures. It emphasizes two additional elements in the yogic practice domain – *japa* or repetition of purifying mantras; and the study of scriptures on spiritual liberation.[11]

Another significant interpretation of this work was the classification of yogis in four categories. Prathamakalpika is the beginner who has practised *vairagya* (detachment) and has acquired the ability to capture the knowledge of others' minds. Madhubhumika is the yogi who is intent on conquering the temptation of the external world and sense organs. This way he obtains *rtambhara prajna* (truth-bearing insight) by listening to scriptures, ability of inference (*anumana*) from this listening and thus enters into practice of dhyana (meditation). Prajnajyoti is the one who, after the conquest of external elements and organs by practising constraint as set forth in the Yoga-Sutras, enters into the state of absolute passionlessness.

The fourth category as delineated by the sage is Atikrantabhavaniya – the one whose only aim is to resolve the mind-wavering and reach the highest state of absolute tranquility in which nothing matters whether external or internal, so that his present life becomes his last. This incidentally corresponds to nirvana as postulated in the Buddhist doctrine.

Notes and References

1. Major available works on Yoga-Sutra are: Patanjali, *The Yoga System of Patanjali or the Ancient Hindu Doctrine of Concentration of Mind*, translated from Sanskrit by James Haughton Woods, Harvard University Press, Cambridge, Massachusetts, 1927 (reprint by Motilal Banarsidass, Delhi, 2005); Patanjala-yoga-sutra-vritti: Yoga-chandika of Narayana-tritha, No. 8984 (serial No. 8010), Asiatic Society, Calcutta; I. K. Taimeni, *The Science of Yoga; A Commentary on the Yoga-sutra of Patanjali in the Light of Modern Thought*, The Theosophical Publication House, Madras (now Chennai),

1961; Georg Feuerstein, *The Yogasutra of Patanjali: An Exercise in the Methodology of Textual Analysis*, Aronld-Herhemann, New Delhi, 1979; Swami Veda Bharati, *Yoga-sutra of Patanjali with the Exposition of Vyasa*, Motilal Banarsidass, Delhi, 2001; and Alistair, Shearer, *The Yoga Sutra of Patanjali*, Dover Publications, New York, 2003.

2. Sures Chandra Banerji, *Studies in Origin and Development of Yoga*, Punthi Pustak, Calcutta (now Kolkata), 1995.

3. S. Radhakrishnan, *Indian Philosophy, Volume-II*, Oxford University Press, New York, 1931, pp. 341–42.

4. The basic commentaries on the Yoga-Sutra are: Yoga Bhashya by Vyasa, Tattva-Vaisharadi by Vachaspati Mishra, Raja-Martanda by Bhojaraja, Patanjala-Rahasya by Raghavananda Saraswati, Yogasutra-gudhartha-dyotika by Narayanendra Sarasvati, and Yoga-siddhanta-candrika and Sutrarthabodhini by Narayana Tirtha.

5. For the text of Goraksa-Sataka, see Akshya Kumar Banerjea, *Philosophy of Gorakhnath*, Motilal Banarsidass, Delhi, 1962; George Western Briggs, *Gorakhnath and the Kanphata Yogis*, Motilal Banarsidass, Delhi, 1982.

6. Briggs, ibid.

7. Banerji, op. cit.

8. Ibid.

9. For the text of the Hatha-yoga-pradipika, see Yogi Hari, *Hatha Yoga Pradipika*, Bookworld Services, Sarasota, Florida, 2005; Pancham Shah, *Hatha Yoga Pradipika*, Bookworld Services,

Sarasota, Florida, 2005; Sures Chandra Banerji, *Studies in Origin and Development of Yoga*, Punthi Pustak, Calcutta, 1995. Also see Usharbudh Arya, *Philosophy of Hatha Yoga*, The Himalayan International Institute of Yoga Science and Philosophy of the USA, Honesdale, 1965. For the evolution of the yoga philosophy of Natha yogis, see Hazari Prasad Dwivedi, *Kabir – A Critical Study* (in Hindi), Rajkamal Prakashan, New Delhi, 1190.

10. Banerji, op. cit.

11. Ganganatha Jha, *Yoga-Darshana: Sutras of Patanjali with Bhasya of Vyasa*, Jain Publishing Company, Fremont, California, 2004; Banerji, op. cit.

Chapter 2

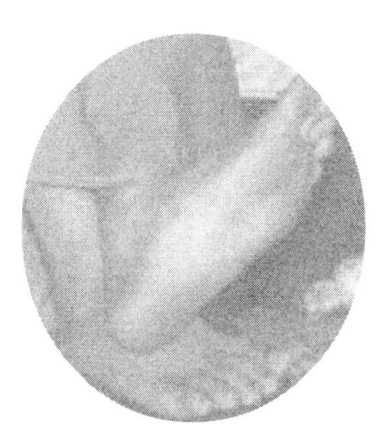

RAMDEV'S PREDECESSORS

... all actions should be performed with the prime objective of benefiting mankind, as opposed to following dogmatic rituals or revering idols and symbols.

Ramdev represents a renewed continuity to the great revival of the ancient Indian spiritual traditions and yoga that took place in the twentieth century and received recognition worldwide. Such towering figures as Sri Aurobindo, Swami Vivekananda, Swami Dayananda, Paramhansa Yogananda, Swami Sahajanand Saraswati, Bhagwan Nityananda, J. N. Krishnamurty and Sri Ramana Rishi had made their way into the national and international consciousness. Demolishing the aberrations and the worst forms of ritualization that had entered the Hindu religion, these men sought to de-pollute the Hindu thought and practices. Their spiritual presence was further enhanced by a host of icons of Indian yoga – Lahiri Mahashaya, Sri Tirumalai Krishnamacharya, Swami Sivananda Saraswati, Swami Kuvalayananda, Shri Yogendra, K. Pattabhi Jois, B. K. S. Iyengar and Swami Satyananda Saraswati – who sought to transform man with an all-encompassing yoga consciousness to heal both body and mind.

These pathfinders evolved their doctrines through a reinterpretation of the ancient wisdom to reconnect spirituality towards the creation of a 'new man' – a spiritually enlightened soul, devoting his newly found energies in the service of society, fighting along the way all kinds of obscurest ideas and practices.

Their missions of enlightenment also focused on reviving a fallen and failed nation caught on the precipice of massive ignorance, directionlessness and a deep alienation from its own spiritual culture. These thinkers created their own vast spiritual space through the celebrated Indian guru–*shishya* tradition, collecting in their crusades thousands of disciples including some of the best minds in other fields – academicians, social workers, bureaucrats and even scientists and medical men.

However, these teachers built their spiritual islands more or less in isolation, propagating their own doctrines and very rarely participating in building a common discourse with their contemporaries. This is notwithstanding their influence on some of the spiritual masters who followed them. This wide diversity in interpretation of the ancient spiritual thought has remained a hallmark of the contribution of our modern spiritual leaders.

The following sections seek to portray the persona of these spiritual yoga icons and the distinguished paths that they laid out for leading a spiritual renaissance. These insights will be used in later chapters to capture the links of Ramdev's legacy with the twentieth century and later spiritual traditions.

The First Three Synergizers of Spiritual Activism

Swami Dayananda Saraswati (1824–83)

Swami Dayananda Saraswati, widely regarded as the foremost authority on the Vedas, was the founder of the Arya Samaj ('Society of Nobles'), a Hindu reform movement set up in 1875. Under his Samaj banner, he launched a powerful crusade against orthodoxy and a host of obscurantist practices of idol worship, animal sacrifices, ancestor worship, pilgrimages, priestcraft, offerings made in temples, the caste system, untouchability, child marriages and discrimination against women, on the grounds that all these lacked Vedic sanction. He discouraged dogma and symbolism, and encouraged scepticism about beliefs that run contrary to common sense and logic. In a sense, the Arya Samaj aimed to be a 'universal church' based on the authority of the Vedas. In its formative years, the Theosophical Society and the Arya Samaj were united under the name Theosophical Society of the Arya Samaj. Unlike many other reform movements within Hinduism, the Arya Samaj's appeal was addressed not only to the educated few in India, but also to the world as a whole, as stated in the sixth principle of the Arya Samaj.[1]

Dayananda was born as Moolshankar into a Brahmin family in 1829, in Tankara village near Morvi (Morbi) in the Kathiawar region of Gujarat. As per his family tradition, he studied Sanskrit, the Vedas and other scriptures to prepare himself for a future as a Hindu priest. However, a number of incidents resulted in young Dayananda questioning the traditional beliefs of Hinduism and enquiring about God. On the night of Shivratri (festival in which God Shiva is worshipped the whole night) when his family went to a temple for overnight worship, he stayed up waiting for God Shiva to appear to accept the offerings made to his idol. While all else slept, Dayananda saw mice eating the offerings kept for the God. He was utterly shocked and wondered how a God, who could not even protect his own 'offerings', would protect humanity. Soon after, two deaths in the family, of his younger sister and his uncle, had a deep impact on the lad. He started pondering over the meaning of life and death, and started asking questions, which worried his parents. They decided to marry him off in his early teens, but like Gautam Buddha, he ran away from home in search of the answers he was seeking so desperately.

After wandering for over two decades all over India, from the caves of Vindhyachal to the Himalayan peaks, he finally found Swami Virjananda, an old blind sanyasi dwelling near Mathura in Uttar Pradesh. The guru trained him in the deeper meaning of the Vedas, and the real meaning of the truth of life. He asked the young seeker to throw away all his books, as their purpose was solved, and get into action. He also gave him the name Rishi Dayananda. The young wandering monk started travelling through villages, towns and cities, delivering the message of the Vedas. He debated with religious pundits and in the presence of thousands of people, made them speechless with his well-articulated arguments.

The seer believed that Hinduism has been corrupted by divergence from the founding principles of the Vedas and misled by the priesthood for the priests' self-aggrandizement. Hindu priests discouraged common folk from reading Vedic scriptures and encouraged rituals (such as bathing in the Ganges and feeding of priests on anniversaries) that Dayananda pronounced as superstitious or self-serving.

Dayananda also emphasized respect and reverence for other human beings, supported by the Vedic notion of the divine nature of the individual. In the ten principles of the Arya Samaj, he enshrined the idea that all actions should be performed with the prime objective of benefiting mankind, as opposed to following dogmatic rituals or revering idols and symbols. In his own life, he interpreted moksha to be a lower calling (due to its benefit to one individual) than the calling to emancipate others.

Swami Dayananda was among the first Indian stalwarts to popularize the concept of Swaraj — the right to self-determination – when India was ruled by the British. His philosophy inspired the nationalists in the Indian uprising of 1857 against the colonizers, as well as freedom fighters such as Lala Lajpat Rai and Bhagat Singh. He was one of the early champions of equal rights for women including their right to education and reading of Indian scriptures, and even had them lead his prayer meetings and lectures.

The seer wrote more than 60 works in all, including a 14-volume explanation of the six Vedangas, an incomplete commentary on the Ashtadhyayi (Panini's grammar), several small texts on ethics and morality, Vedic rituals and sacraments, and critiques of rival doctrines (such as Advaita Vedanta). He founded the Paropakarini Sabha located at Ajmer in Rajasthan to publish his works and Vedic texts. Some of his famous works are: Satyarth Prakash (Light on Truth), Rigvedadi Bhashya Bhumika (Introduction to Vedas), Rigveda Bhashya and Yajurveda Bhashya (Introduction to Commentary on Vedas), and Sanskar Vidhi. Dayananda's Vedic doctrine influenced many thinkers. It is said that Sri Aurobindo decided to explore the hidden psychological meanings of the Vedas after studying his works.

The great social reformer was poisoned in 1883 while a guest of the maharaja of Jodhpur. On his deathbed, he forgave his killer, the maharaja's cook, and actually gave him money to flee the king's wrath.

Swami Vivekananda (1863–1902)

Swami Vivekananda is hailed as one of India's most charismatic spiritual leaders who, like Swami Dayananda, sought to promote the spiritual synergy of an awakening nation with the ideals of social transformation. At the same time, he became a forerunner in establishing the lost glory of Indian spiritualism in the eyes of the world.[2]

Born on 12 January 1863, as Narendra Nath in a rich attorney family of Calcutta, Vivekananda was the heir apparent of his guru, Ramakrishna. After his guru's death in 1886, the responsibility of managing the monastery at Baranagore fell upon him. But he did not want to be imprisoned within the four walls of a monastery; rather, he longed to study India first hand. He travelled all over northern and western India before turning south. He found his true enlightenment in December 1892 while sitting in meditation on a rock at Cape Comorin in Kanyakumari. He envisioned a transformation of India by spiritually raising its masses for national reconstruction and bringing back its self-prestige.

In 1893, Vivekananda went to America to gather resources for his mission and also to bring the Vedanta to the attention of the West. At the Parliament of Religions held in the Hall of Columbus at the Arts Institute in Chicago, he started his passionate speech by addressing the gathering as 'sisters and brothers of America'! The effect was electrifying. The whole audience stood up to a man, cheering and waving wildly for minutes. Annie Besant wrote long after: 'The large multitude hung upon his words enraptured. Not a cadence missed. "That man a heathen!" said one, as he came out of the great hall, and we send missionaries to his people! It would be more fitting that they should send missionaries to us.'

After his return from the West, Vivekananda founded Ramakrishna Mission in 1897 to propagate the ideals of personal salvation and to promote the use of mass spiritual consciousness for the uplift of the poor in the country. The mission began its work by starting famine-relief centres in Murshidabad district. Soon it set up a large number of schools, orphanages and dispensaries. Meanwhile, Vivekananda kept preaching the message of spiritual development, fearlessness and social action until his death on 4 July 1902, at the young age of 39.

The Vivekananda Kendra was started in the year 1972 with the aim of popularizing the teachings of the swami. It has about 170 branch centres spread over 18 states of India, teaching yoga and meditation, and carrying out a host of social-service activities.

Swami Sahajanand Saraswati (1889–1950)

Swami Sahajanand Saraswati, one of the most fascinating mass figures in modern history, was the foremost leader of the peasantry in Bihar. A saffron-clad sanyasi-turned-Gandhian, and then a communist and finally a peasant leader, this avant-gardist was a true iconoclast, demolishing in one go all opportunistic and self-aggrandizing ideologies of his times.

Sahajanand was born as Naurang Rai in 1889 to a family of Bhumihar Brahmins, in Ghazipur district in eastern Uttar Pradesh. He studied at the German Mission high school. He was a restless lad, and his family often found him thinking of renouncing the world to find real spiritual solace. To prevent him from doing this, his family had him married to a child bride, but within a year his wife died. In 1907, Naurang Rai joined the holy order with the name that was soon to find fame.

Sahajanand began his political career by organizing his own Bhumihar Brahmin community, but soon joined the Nationalist Congress politics and became a devoted follower of Mahatma Gandhi. He remained a formidable Congress activist for 15 years, but later got disgusted with the petty, comfort-seeking hypocrisy of the self-proclaimed Gandhians, especially in jail.

He also got disillusioned with Gandhi's own ambiguity and pro-propertied attitudes. In 1934, during the relief operations in the aftermath of the great earthquake in Bihar, he was extremely perturbed by the cruelty of the landlords in rent collection amidst such horrifying calamity. Sahajanand went to meet Gandhi, who was then camping at Patna, to ask for advice. Gandhi sanguinely told him that the zamindars would remove the difficulties of the peasants. Their managers were Congressmen and, hence, they would definitely help the poor. But the swami found no end to the oppression of the peasantry. Then onwards, he consistently saw the Mahatma as a wily politician who, in order to defend the propertied classes, took recourse in pseudo-spiritualism, profession of non-violence and religious hocus-pocus.

In the third phase of his career, Sahajanand emerged as the foremost *kisan* leader in India and formed the All India Kisan Sabha with the Congress Socialists. He joined Subhas Chandra Bose to organize the Anti-Compromise Conference against the British and the Congress. He worked with the Communist Party of India as well during the Second World War, but ultimately broke away from them, too. He was relentlessly determined to improve the peasants' condition and pursued that objective with such force and energy that he was almost universally loved by the peasants, and both respected and feared by landlords, Congressmen and officials.

The swami established an ashram at Neyamatpur, Gaya (Bihar), which later became the centre of the freedom struggle in Bihar. He died on 26 June 1950. Like his contemporary spiritual and social activists, he was also a prolific writer. His autobiography, *Mera Jeewan Sangharsha* (My Life Struggle), in Hindi is hailed as one of the most important reference materials on the history of pre-independent India. His other works include *Kranti aur Samyukta Morcha, Kisanon ke Dave, Jhootha Bhay Mithya Abhiman* (False Fear False Pride), *Brahman Kaun?, Brahmarshi Vansha Vistar* in Sanskrit, Hindi and English, and *Karmakalap* in Sanskrit and Hindi. His selected works have been published in six volumes.[3]

The Reinventors of Yoga

Lahiri Mahashaya (1828–98)

Lahiri Mahashaya was a great proponent of Kriya Yoga. The Kriya yogi mentally directs his life energy to revolve, upward and downward, around the six spinal centers that correspond to the 12 astral signs of the zodiac, the symbolic Cosmic Man. Half a minute of revolution of energy around the sensitive spinal cord of man effects subtle progress in his evolution; that half-minute of Kriya equals one year of natural spiritual unfolding.

The world first heard about Lahiri Mahashaya from Paramahansa Yogananda's *Autobiography of a Yogi*.[4] Born as Shyama Lahiri, this yogi, unlike other spiritual masters, was a family man, and worked as an accountant in the Military Engineering Department of the British Government. He lived with his family at Varanasi – rather than all alone in a monastery.

The spiritual turnaround in his life took place when he was 33 years old. In 1861, he was stationed at the foothills of the Himalayas as part of his job and there he became a disciple of Mahavatar Babaji, a great Himalayan yogi and a master of Kriya Yoga. The guru directed his disciple to return to worldly life and popularize his yoga among people. Lahiri Mahashaya also worked against the caste system and for the emancipation of women.

Sri Tirumalai Krishnamacharya (1888–1989)

Sri Tirumalai Krishnamacharya, one of the early yoga icons of India, was a forerunner in establishing a distinguished tradition of yoga which produced many of today's most influential teachers: B. K. S. Iyengar, the late K. Pattabhi Jois, the late Indra Devi, Srivatsa Ramaswami, A. G. Mohan, and Krishnamacharya's own son T. K. V. Desikachar.[5]

Krishnamacharya was born on 18 November 1888 in Muchukundapuram, in Chitradurga district of Karnataka, to an Iyengar family of distinguished ancestry. Among his forebears was the ninth-century teacher and sage Nathamuni, who was acknowledged as a great teacher and an author of remarkable works, such as the Nyaya Tattva. Krishnamacharya's father was a well-known teacher of the Vedas. At the age of six, he underwent *upanayana* and began learning Sanskrit, Vedas and other texts such as the Amarakosha under the strict tutelage of his father.

After his father's death, the family had to move to Mysore, where Krishnamacharya's great-grandfather, Sri Srinivasa Brahmatantra Parakala Swami, was the head of the Parakala Matha. The young lad completed formal schooling at the Chamaraj Sanskrit College and in the *matha*. He passed his Vidvan examination in Vedic scholarship in Mysore, where he had studied *vyakarana*, Vedanta and *tarka*. At the age of 16 he started travelling through India, studying during his travels the six *darsana*s or Indian philosophies: Vaisesika, Nyaya, Sankhya, Yoga, Mimamsa and Vedanta. In 1906, he reached Benares University and continued his studies in logic and Sanskrit, working with Brahmashri Shivakumar Shastry, one of the greatest grammarians of the period. In 1909, he returned to Mysore and studied Vedanta at the Parakala Matha. During this period he learned to play the vina, one of the most ancient Indian stringed instruments.

In 1914, he once again left for Benares and the Queen's College. During the first year, as he had no financial support from his family; he got his food by following the rules that were laid down for religious beggars: approaching seven households each day and offering a prayer in return for wheat flour to mix with water for cakes. From Benaras, our scholar joined Patna University to re-study the shad-darsana (six *darsana*s) of the Vedic philosophy. He got a scholarship to study Ayurveda under Vaidya Krishnakumar of Bengal. He also learnt yoga from Shri Babu Bhagwan Das, and passed the Sankhya Yoga Examination of Patna.

In 1919, Krishnamacharya went in search of Yogeshwara Ramamohan Brahmachari, a yoga master who was rumoured to live in the Himalayas beyond Nepal. When he sought permission from the viceroy, Lord Irwin (Edward Frederick Lindley Wood), the latter asked him to cure his diabetes. Krishnamacharya taught him yogic practices for six months. Pleased with the results, the viceroy made arrangements for his travel to Tibet, supplying three aides and taking care of the expenses. Eventually, Krishnamacharya found Sri Brahmachari dwelling in a cave at the foot of Mount Kailash. He spent seven-and-a-half years studying the Yoga-Sutras of Patanjali, learning asanas and pranayama, and studying the therapeutic aspects of yoga. He was also made to memorize the whole of the Yoga Kuruntha in the Gurkha language.

After his return to southern India, Krishnamacharya kept studying Ayurveda as well as Nyaya, a school of Indian philosophy concerned with logic and epistemology. Finally, in 1924, he opened a yoga school under the patronage of the maharaja of Mysore. There, he taught until 1955 and wrote several books including *Yoga Makaranda, Yoganjali* and *Yogasanalu.* He got married in 1925. Meanwhile, he was forced to take up a job as a foreman at a coffee plantation since he was unwilling to fall under the obligation of the maharaja.

Krishnamacharya's yoga doctrine was built around Ashtanga Vinyasa Yoga, with emphasis on a vigorous style aimed at building strength and stamina. He particularly stressed the importance of combining breath work (pranayama) with the postures (asanas) and meditation to reach the desired goal. He was also a physician of Ayurvedic medicine and had vast knowledge of nutrition, herbal medicine, the use of oils, and other remedies. The seer was perhaps the first yoga master who never emphasized the religious aspect of yoga, so that people of all communities – Muslims, Christians and others – came to study yoga under him. He always took time to understand the religion and the culture of the people he taught. When the Nizam of Hyderabad invited the master to teach him, he spoke to him in Urdu. The Nizam was so impressed that his entire family started practising yoga. Krishnamacharya never left India over the course of his life.

At the age of 96, he suffered from fracture of the hip. He refused surgery and treated himself by designing a course of yoga practice that he could do in bed. Krishnamacharya died in 1989 at the age of 100 years. On his death, writer Fernando Pages Ruiz said: 'Whether you practice the dynamic series of Pattabhi Jois, the refined alignments of B. K. S. Iyengar, the classical postures of Indra Devi, or the customized vinyasa of Viniyoga, your practice stems from one source: a

Baba Ramdev with his parents (on the extreme right) among others

Baba celebrating Holi with his devotees in Patna

Thousands of Baba's followers at one of his yoga camps

Baba regularly teaches yoga to children

Baba blessing a devotee

A devotee blessing Baba

Baba in a meditative mood during his teachings

Baba offering prayers to the sun

five-foot, two-inch Brahmin born more than one hundred years ago in a small South Indian village.'

Swami Sivananda Saraswati (1887–1963)

Swami Sivananda, a doctor-turned-yogi, was among the spiritual icons who promoted the doctrine of yoga all over the world. A leading proponent of Nishkamya Karma Yoga, he stressed the ideal of selfless service, which promotes preparatory purification for the higher consciousness. His yoga package included Karma Yoga; Bhakti Yoga, the yoga of love or devotion; Jnana Yoga, the yoga of wisdom; Raja Yoga; and Mantra Yoga.[6]

Born Kuppuswamy Iyer on 8 September 1887 in the village of Pattamadai in South India, Swami Sivananda studied at Tanjore Medical College and practised at Tiruchi. After the death of his father in 1913, he transferred his practice to Malaysia, working as in-charge of a hospital on a rubber estate. Under the tutelage of a wandering sadhu, he started studying Hindu scriptures and the Bible. In 1923, the young doctor returned to India, gave away his possessions, and spent a year on pilgrimage to holy places. At Rishikesh, he was initiated by Swami Viswananda Saraswati as Swami Sivananda Saraswati. He kept working as a doctor, looking after sick monks and pilgrims. In 1927, he set up a charitable dispensary from the money he received for a matured insurance policy, and gave packets of medicines to pilgrims as they passed the dispensary on their way to Badrinath.

In 1932, the master founded the Sivananda Ashram, and four years later the Divine Life Society and an in-house journal, *The Divine Life*. In 1945, he set up the Sivananda Ayurvedic Pharmacy to make drugs from rare Himalayan herbs. In 1948, he established the Yoga-Vedanta Forest Academy to impart training to disciples and the laity. The Sivananda Eye Hospital opened in 1957. Today, there are many thousands of followers of Swami Sivananda all over the world, with more than 137 branches of the Divine Life Society in India, the United States of America, Canada, Bahamas, South America, Australia, Europe and South Africa. *Yoga Life Magazine* is published by the International Sivananda Yoga Vedanta Centers twice a year.

Swami Sivananda passed away in 1963, and his chief disciple – Swami Chidananda – became president of the Divine Life Society and led its rapid spread in the West through his world tours. His other disciples who built new organizations are Swami Chinmayananda, the founder of the Chinmaya Mission; Swami Jyotirmayananda, president of the Yoga Research Foundation in Miami, USA; Swami Satchidananda, founder of the Integral Yoga Institutes, USA; and Swami Satyananda Saraswati, the founder of Satyananda Yoga Mission.

Swami Kuvalayananda (1883–1966)

Swami Kuvalayananda, the famous pioneer of the scientific study of Hatha Yoga, contributed in several ways in the fields of scientific, literary and therapeutic research in yoga and yoga education.

He was born as Jagannath Ganesh Gune into a Marathi family on 30 August 1883, at Dabhoi in Baroda district. A noted scholar, educationist and national freedom fighter, he set up the Khandesh Education Society in 1916 and worked as the principal of the society's college (1921–23). As an adolescent, Gune become a student of Paramahamsa Shree Madhavadasji Maharaj of the yoga centre at Malsar, on the banks of the river Narmada in Gujarat.[7]

In 1943, Kuvalayananda set up twin organizations – Kaivalyadhama Ashram with emphasis on spiritual development, and Kaivalyadhama Sreeman Madhava Yoga Mandir (SMYM) at Lonavala, Poona (now Pune), specializing in the medical and scientific investigation of yoga. He also established Gorhandas Seksaria College of Yoga and Cultural Synthesis to train young men and women in the special art and science of yoga.

Kaivalyadhama, Lonavala, offers yoga classes and workshops, and yogic therapy for different ailments. It also offers an advanced teachers' training course in yoga. It has several branches in India and two branches in the United States and France. Since 1935, the Kaivalyadhama SMYM Samhiti has been publishing a journal titled *Yoga-Mimamsa*.

Shri Yogendra (1897–1989)

Shri Yogendra was one of the early spiritual masters who led the revival of classical yoga by rescuing it from the dark caverns of hermits and placing it at the doorsteps of the common man. Born on 18 November 1897, he renounced his family when he was still an adolescent to follow his guru, Paramahamsa Madhavadasaji, a renowned yogi living at Malsar in Gujarat. After completing his training, he decided to leave the ashram, in order to propagate the benefits of yoga amongst the masses.[8]

In 1918, Shri Yogendra established the Yoga Institute at Versova, Mumbai, at the house of M. M. Masani, a renowned social activist. Masani offered his place since he was impressed with the yogi's poetry. A year later, Yogendra went to the United States, where he opened a branch of the institute in New York.

Despite being a yogi, Shri Yogendra got married in 1927. His wife, Sitadevi, also become a proponent of yoga and worked towards promoting yoga among women. She authored *Yoga Simplified for Women*,[9] the first authoritative book on yoga for women written by a woman. Sitadevi faced immense criticism not only because she was a woman doing yoga, but also because she was the wife of a yogi.

Shri Yogendra presented yoga to the world as the art of living acquired with physical, mental, moral, intellectual, emotional and spiritual discipline, and ordained that it must be studied with an open mind. He carried several innovations in classical yoga to suit common people. These include developing a breathing rhythm that accompanies yogic postures and simplifications of yoga postures without diminishing their benefits. According to him, there are four basic elements that one needs to understand in yoga: dharma (sense of duty), *jnana* (awareness), *vairagya* (objectivity with detachment) and *aishwarya* (attainment). Shri Yogendra died in 1989, passing on his legacy to his son, Dr Jayadev Yogendra.

K. Pattabhi Jois (1915–2009)

K. Pattabhi Jois, a short, barrel-chested man with twinkling eyes and a bright smile, was a proponent of Ashtanga Yoga. He was an early disciple of T. Krishnamacharya.[10]

Jois was born in 1915 in the village of Kowshika, near Hassan, Karnataka. His father was a priest and a landholder, and had taught the young lad Sanskrit and various rituals preparing him for priesthood in future. In 1927, at the age of 12, he became a disciple of T. Krishnamacharya, but never told his family that he was learning yoga. He would rise early, go to practice, and then go to school. In 1930, he ran away from home to Mysore and joined Krishnamacharya's *yoga-shala* as his assistant. Jois would often accompany his teacher on yoga discourses he conducted on invitation. He also studied texts such as Patanjali's Yoga-Sutras, Hatha-yoga-pradipika, Suta-Samhita, Yoga-Yajnavalkya and the Upanishads. After his marriage in 1937, he joined the faculty of Sanskrit College as a lecturer of yoga. In 1948, he established the Ashtanga Yoga Research Institute.

Jois came to be known to the Western world in 1967, when André Van Lysebeth from Belgium became his student and published a book called *J'apprends le Yoga* (1967, *Yoga Self-Taught* in English). Soon a large number of foreigners started coming to Mysore to study yoga under the masters. His new followers included celebrities such as singer-musicians Madonna, Sting and Gwyneth Paltrow.

From 1974 onwards, Jois made several trips to the United States teaching Ashtanga Yoga. He wrote his only book, *Yoga Mala*, in Kannada in 1958; it was not published in English until 1999.[11] *Guru*, a film on his life, was made by Robert Wilkins.

Jois's yoga practice regimen is built around a complete synchronization of breath and body movement, called *vinyasa*, derived from an ancient yogic text called the Yoga-Korunta. It is designed to stoke the inner fires and generate *tapa* or resilience in a yogi's practice. It regulates and enhances the flow of prana in body. It also calms the mind through generating *samata*, thus creating a state of mind conducive to meditation while in action. The book, *Ashtanga Yoga – The Definitive Step-by-Step Guide to Dynamic Yoga*[12] based on Jois's method has been hailed as one of the best manuals on yoga.

Like his fellow master Iyengar, Jois was a strict disciplinarian with a gentle touch. He rebuked any student who was not calm and collected. He believed that asking too many questions reflected an agitated frame of mind, and through practice alone will the mind be calmed and tamed. He also refused to talk about tantra, mantra, kundalini, or yoga philosophy. Unlike the sprawling yoga campuses of other gurus, the Ashtanga Yoga Institute operates from a tiny concrete-floored room at Jois's home in Mysore. The master passed away on 18 May 2009 at the age of 93.

B. K. S. Iyengar (1918–)

B. K. S. Iyengar, the living yoga legend, known the world over with his brand Iyengar Yoga, has to his claim nearly four million disciples across the world, a performance record of 10,000 live lecture demonstrations, and even a star named after him. His book, *Light on Yoga*, has sold over a million copies across the world. Apart from the celebrated violinist, Yehudi Menuhin, his students include the late J. N. Krishnamurti, Aldous Huxley and several heads of European states.[13]

Born in 1918 into a poor family in a small village in Karnataka, Iyengar was initiated into yoga at the age of 15 by the legendary yoga guru, Krishnamacharya. He had to endure his taskmaster guru's stinging reproaches and beating through ten-hour practice sessions every day. Finally, the teacher, pleased with his acumen, awarded him with a gold medal inscribed with the words '*Yoganga Sikshaka Chakravarti*' ('king among yoga teachers').

In 1937, Iyengar moved to Pune and joined Deccan Gymkhana Club as a yoga instructor. Despite immense financial hardships, he started his own private yoga school. Iyengar's lingering career witnessed a sudden flip in 1952 when Yehudi Menuhin, on a visit to India, was highly impressed by his healing powers. He asked him to introduce yoga to the world. And since that time, Iyengar has made innumerable trips around the world, popularizing the science and philosophy of yoga. In 1982, on an invitation by the educational department of the United Kingdom, he participated in the Festival of India, London.

Iyengar's yoga is built around yogic postures (which he disarmingly calls 'poses'). Apart from asanas, Iyengar is also a master of the eight limbs of yoga enunciated in Patanjali's Yoga-Sutras: *yamas* and *niyamas* (dos and don'ts), pranayama (breath control), *pratyahara* (sense withdrawal), *dharana* (one-pointedness), dhyana (meditation) and samadhi (union with universal consciousness). The purists, however, are against his violation of the tradition of one-to-one teaching. They also accuse Iyengar of glorifying the body and converting yoga from a way of life to a physical culture. Apart from *Light on Yoga*, the master has also authored *Light on the Yoga Sutras of Patanjali* published in 1993.

Iyengar, a true yoga scientist, has brought about several innovations in yoga healing system – a wide set of props such as ropes, benches, bandages and wooden bricks. The guru is also a hard taskmaster and even hits his students physically. He says, 'There's a skill in my hitting. I use it to move the skin and help them get a better pose.' Iyengar also refuses to engage his followers in the dreary debates on self-realization and emancipation. In an interview, when he was asked whether he was enlightened, he retorted, 'Do I have to boast? I have not been to school or college. Yet I've written books and addressed universities. Is that not enlightenment? Yoga gave me the ability to see my body as my small self, and my soul as my infinite self.'

The startling healing power of Iyengar's yoga has been widely established by a number of case studies. Nivedita Joshi, daughter of Indian politician Murli Manohar Joshi, got cured of a damaged spine from which she had been suffering for 12 years. Zippora Weiner from Israel, who was blown up in a land mine and struggled for life for more than eight months, found a new lease of life in the hands of the master. In his foreword to *Light on Yoga*, Yehudi Menuhin pays a tribute to Iyengar's prowess, 'Whoever has had the privilege of receiving Mr Iyengar's attention, or of witnessing the precision and beauty of his art, is introduced to that vision of perfection and innocence which is man as first created – unarmed, unashamed, son of God – in the Garden of Eden.'

Swami Satyananda Saraswati (1923–)

Swami Satyananda Saraswati, the founder of the Bihar School of Yoga, was a proponent of systematic practices of yoga and brought in new combinations of yogic techniques. He also incorporated various components of tantra in the yogic system. His key contribution is Yoga Nidra, the revised version of the tantric system of *nyasa* meditation that helps energize various parts of the body by specific mantras (chants); and the *pawana-muktasana* series of asanas for rheumatic problems and gastric problems and *shakti bandha* or postures to release energies within the body.[14]

Swami Satyananda was born in 1923 in Almora in the Himalayan foothills, in a landed family. When he reached the age of 19, he took *sanyas* under the tutelage of Swami Sivananda at Sivananda Ashram in Rishikesh. He edited the ashram's Hindi journal, wrote various articles and composed poems in both Hindi and Sanskrit. He wrote a translation and a commentary in English of the Brihadaranyaka Upanishad by Swami Sivananda.

In 1955, he left the ashram and travelled through India, Afghanistan, Nepal, Burma and Ceylon (now Sri Lanka) for the next eight years, enhancing his knowledge of various spiritual traditions. He set up the Bihar Yoga School in 1963 in order to carry out the mission assigned to him by his guru to spread the message of yoga in the country. Recognizing the global resurgence of yoga in the 1970s, he founded the International Yoga Fellowship. Specialized yoga training for industrial and corporate houses also became a part of Bihar School's regular activities. In 1984, Swami Satyananda established the Sivananda Math, dedicated to the memory of his guru, Swami Satyananda, through which students are regularly sent to villages in and around Munger and other parts of Bihar to help uplift the condition of the common people. In 1988, he retired from active involvement in yoga teaching and handed over the active work of his ashram to his chief disciple, Swami Niranjanananda.

Notes and References

1. Swami Dayanand, *Satyarath Prakash*, Arya Pratinidhi Sabha, New Delhi, 1984; Glyn Richards, *A Source-Book of Modern Hinduism*, Curzon Press, London, 1985; Noel Anthony Salmond, *Hindu Iconoclasts: Rammohun Roy, Dayananda Sarasvati and Nineteenth-Century Polemics against Idolatry*, Wilfrid Laurier University Press, Waterloo, Canada, 2004; Arvind Sharma, *Modern Hindu Thought*, Oxford University Press, New Delhi, 2002.

2. Swami Vivekananda, *Complete Works of Swami Vivekananda*, Volume I, Advaita Ashrama, Mayavati, Almora, 2001; Y. Masih, *Introduction to Religious Philosophy*, Motilal Banarsidass, Delhi, 1991; Arun Kumar Biswas, *Swami Vivekananda and the Indian Quest for Socialism*, Firma KLM Private Ltd, Calcutta, 1985.

3. Swami Sahajanand, *Mera Jeewan Sangharsha* (My Life Struggle), in Hindi, Peoples' Publication House, New Delhi, 1952; Walter Hauser, *Swami Sahajanand and the Peasants of Jharkhand: A View from 1941*, translated from Hindi, Manohar Publishers, New Delhi, 2005; Swami Sahajanand Saraswati, *Rachnawali* (Selected Works of Swami Sahajanand Saraswati) in six volumes, Prakashan Sansthan, Delhi, 2003.

4. Paramahansa Yogananda, *Autobiography of a Yogi*, Crystal Clarity Publishers, Nevada City, California, 2005 (reprint of 1946; first edition published by Philosophical Library, New York).

5. Kausthub Desikachar, *The Yoga of the Yogi: The Legacy of T. Krishnamacharya*, Krishnamacharya Yoga Mandiram, Chennai, 2005.

6. Swami Venkatesananda, *Sivananda: Biography of a Modern Sage*, Divine Life Society, Rishikesh, Haridwar, 1985.

7. Swami Kuvalayananda, *Asanas*, Yoga-Mimamsa Office, Lonavala, 1972; M. L. Gharote and M. M. Gharote, *Swami Kuvalayananda: A Pioneer of Scientific Yoga and Physical Education*, Manohar Publishers, New Delhi, 2004.

8. Shri Yogendra, *Yoga Physical Education (for Men)*, Yoga Institute, Bombay (now Mumbai), 1947.

9. Sitadevi, *Yoga Simplified for Women*, Yoga Institute, Bombay (now Mumbai), 1938.

10. Eddie Stern and Deirdre Summerbell, *Sri K. Pattabhi Jois: A Tribute*, Eddie Stern and Gwyneth Paltrow, New York, 2002.

11. K. Pattabhi Jois, *Yoga Mala*, North Point Press, New York, 1999.

12. John C. Scott, *Ashtanga Yoga – The Definitive Step-by-Step Guide to Dynamic Yoga*, Three Rivers Press, New York, 2001.

13. B. K. S. Iyengar, *Iyengar – His Life and Work*, C. B. S. Publishers & Distributors, 1991; B. K. S. Iyengar, *Light on Yoga* (1964), (revised edition) Schocken Books, New York, 1995.

14. Swami Niranjanananda Saraswati, *The Growth of Satyananda Yoga or Bihar Yoga*, (January) Yoga Ganga Darshan, Munger, Bihar, 2000.

Chapter 3

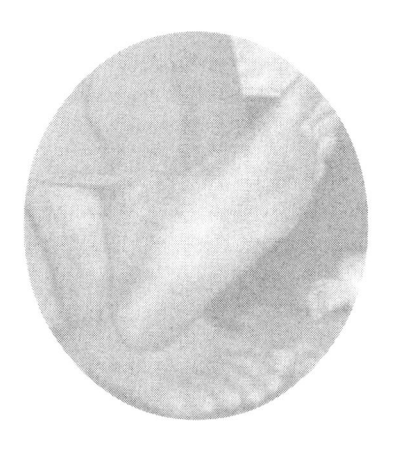

RAMDEV'S PATH OF SELF-DISCOVERY
AND YOGA-HEALING PHILOSOPHY

प्रतिपल भगवान की कृपा का अनुभव करें

The key constituent of Ramdev's yoga doctrine, which differentiates his yoga from the classical yoga traditionally propounded by his predecessors as well as contemporaries, is the overbearing emphasis on pranayama. While the yoga traditions so far have focused on yogasanas, this technique was not given much importance. According to Ramdev, ... while pranayamas strengthen the software of the body, asanas empower its hardware.

Not much is known about Swami Ramdev's early life. He believes that after a person has renounced the world, there is no distinction between the family of his birth and the entire humanity, as the humanity becomes his family. However, a rough sketch of his early life can be drawn from what he has occasionally revealed in his discourses.[1] He was born perhaps in 1965 as Ramkishan Yadav in an illiterate family of Narnaul village at Alipur in Mahendragarh district of Haryana. He studied at the village school till fifth class and made his mark as the brightest student there. He then moved to another school in a nearby village, Shahjadpur, where he completed his eighth class. Since there was no electricity in the village, he studied in kerosene lamplight. His only study material was second-hand books purchased by his father. His family includes his parents, a brother and a sister, but he does not interact much with them.

Ramdev's childhood had an abiding influence on his future life. As a child he was afflicted by paralysis of the left side. According to him, it was through yoga that he was able to regain the full functioning and shape of his body. In all likelihood, child Ramdev's paralytic condition and its cure by yoga must have induced in him a gradual distancing from the usual rhythm of life. This unusual experience might have evoked in him an urge to push his life onto a path that could lead him to the roots of knowledge, and to the true purpose of his very existence. Soon, the lad would have started seeking the ultimate freedom and a socially useful role, beyond the yoke of family, community and formal education, and the need to build a livelihood. As he recalls later, 'I learnt early in life that there were deep imbalances in health, education and wealth distribution in the country.' Thus, a pilgrim's progress had begun for the child with all its hindrances and uncertainties.

The first turning point in young Ramdev's spiritual career occurred when he quit home and joined a yogic monastery (*gurukul*) set up by Acharya Baldev in Khanpur village in Kishangarh Ghaseda, in Rewari district of Haryana. The *acharya* facilitated the youngster's exposure to Panini's Sanskrit grammar and knowledge of the Vedas and Upanishads. At the same time, he also started practising intense self-discipline and meditation. Although not formally associated with the Arya Samaj, he was greatly influenced by the ideals of Swami Dayananda in these formative years.

Ramdev renounced the world and donned the robe of a sanyasi (one who takes up monastic living), and assumed the name, Swami Ramdev. He recalls, 'I did not become a sanyasi due to some inspiration or influence of others. I wanted to be a sanyasi when I was only four years old. I never had the escapist mentality.' He then moved to Jind district of Haryana, where he joined the Gurukul Kalva headed by Acharya Dharamveer and started offering free yoga teaching to villagers across Haryana.

Ramdev's quest, however, was not yet complete. Like several earlier spiritual masters, his wandering mind forced him to move on to the Himalayas, where he spent years visiting various ashrams, thereby further expanding his understanding of yoga and meditation being practised by the sages there. One day, during deep meditation in a cave near the Gangotri glacier, he finally reached the desired enlightenment, realizing vividly the true mission of his life which he was trying to comprehend all those years. 'When I was in the Himalayas, I used to think a lot; there was an internal conflict going on in my mind. I used to think, "What I am doing here? Sanyasi fraternity is for the welfare of the mankind. If my life ends in this place, then whatever little knowledge I have, will also end with me,"' he recalls. There, he also met his future compatriots, Acharya Balkrishna and Acharya Karamveer, who were to become his invaluable partners in the mission he was to soon set upon. At the same place, he also met Acharya Muktananda and Acharya Virendra, also his future collaborators.

In 1993, Ramdev left the Himalayas and came to Haridwar. In 1995, he became a disciple of Swami Shankar Dev, the head of Kripalu Bagh Ashram. The ashram was set up in 1932 by Swami Kripalu Dev, a revolutionary-turned-spiritual master. Born as Yati Kishore Chand in Mewar, Rajasthan, he went on to become an active freedom fighter. He was a member of the Bang Viplav Dal formed by the revolutionaries in Bengal and had the responsibility of circulating the newspapers, *Yugantar* and *Lokantar* in northern India. These newspapers acted as the voice of the freedom fighters and were banned by the British Government, which made several attempts to locate the place of publishing and distribution of these papers, but failed repeatedly.

Kishore Chand gave refuge to several freedom fighters including the legendary Rash Behari Bose, who was involved in the Lord Hardinge bomb episode and on whom the British Government had announced a reward of three lakh rupees. Kishore Chand is also credited with setting up of the first public library of Haridwar which had an impressive collection of about

3,500 books. He established several schools in the region to impart education in a nationalist framework and create a solid support base for the freedom movement among the youth.

During this period, Kishore Chand took sanyas and subsequently came to be known as Swami Kripalu Dev. He was a close associate of Bal Gangadhar Tilak, Madan Mohan Malviya, Motilal Nehru, Mahatma Gandhi, Chittaranjan Das, Ganesh Shankar Vidyarthi, V. J. Patel, Hakim Ajmal Khan, Jawaharlal Nehru, Shyama Prasad Mukherjee, Purushottam Das Tandon and Swami Shraddhananda, the founder of Gurukul Kangdi University. They often used to visit the ashram.

Swami Kripalu Dev published the magazine *Vishva Gyan* which acted as a mouthpiece of the freedom movement. He wrote several books including *Vedagita Saar*, *Jivanmudra Gita* and *Atmabrahma Bodhmala*. He died in 1968 at the age of 100. Swami Shankar Dev became his successor.

In 1995, after taking *diksha* from his guru, Ramdev launched a low-keyed mission of spreading yoga and its medicinal benefits among people. He used to walk on the streets of Haridwar distributing pamphlets articulating the importance of yoga and Ayurveda. He also began experimenting with yoga on the human body, and after a detailed research over a period of more than five years, he finally established his now-world-famous yoga health doctrine. He revealed this doctrine at his first public meeting in 2002. Yoga treatment camps were started in 2003 and the first residential camp was put in place in the following year. It seems that Ramdev announced his arrival after extensive preparations. He is reported to have learnt English and had also taken up long lessons on modern medical science and the treatment methods for various diseases from well-qualified allopathic doctors. As his discourses later showed, his study and understanding of medical terminology and nature of diseases and drug therapy is striking.

Yoga and Healing Philosophy

Ramdev has built his yoga doctrine around the spiritual tenets of Patanjali's Yoga-Sutras, Gorakhnath's Goraksa-Sataka and Swami Swatamarama's Hatha-yoga-pradipika. This doctrine represents the first-ever attempt towards demystifying yoga for the common man through a simplified reinterpretation of the yoga philosophy of these ancient seers, keeping in context today's requirements of health care. Holding that twentieth-century medical science has completely failed to build a disease-free man, Ramdev proposes to establish yoga as the mainstream health-care system. According to him, the yoga way of life leads to health, which cannot be obtained from somebody's blessings or service but is the result of changes brought about within oneself by realizing the truth of yoga.

This realization, he says, brings in changes in lifestyle, attitude and behaviour. Asserting that 'health is the fundamental right of all human beings', he has pronounced his ultimate aim 'to make every individual healthy, disease free and happy, and stop the death of even a single person due to illness'. According to the seer, man is unhappy and distanced from peace because he has forgotten the very idea of well-being amid the pulls of a materialist culture. Yoga is the best vehicle to discover and realize one's Self, pure consciousness and internal brightness. Ramdev also insists that the correct way to pronounce 'yoga' is '*yog*', as is done in Sanskrit and Hindi.

According to Ramdev's philosophy, yoga helps in mastering concentration of the mind inflicted with *smriti* or memory of past experience and ideas. The mind has three qualities – *raj*, *tama* and *satva*. *Raj* or anger is action and behaviour. When the mind is awake, it is full of *raj* quality, which diverts the mind towards action on a temporary basis with the support of *tama* (passions) and *satva* (chaste state). *Tama's* chief characteristic is stationary state or stability, and blocks light and action, while *satva* has the opposite manifestation.

The seer, in his attempt towards demystification of yoga, has drawn from the classical yoga texts the essential elements of Hatha Yoga, while completely ignoring in his popular discourses the complex rendering on the metaphysical aspects of kundalini samadhi and siddhis, which the classical texts hail as the ultimate goals of a yogi par excellence. Yet, like the ancient yoga founders, Ramdev extols Hatha Yoga as a branch of science that seeks to establish the conduct of human body in the domain of spiritual energy movement and distribution principle, which has remained far beyond the comprehension of modern medical science. As discussed earlier, the body–energy dynamics, according to the sages, is based on a balance of two energy streams – the fire energy – Pingala – or the solar *nadi* in the subtle body, representing strength, courage, bravery and valour, and the pious energy – Ida – or the lunar *nadi*. These two operate in a dialectical relationship and the task of a practitioner is to bring about a synthesis of the two, which eventually leads to devotion, calm, peace, patience, harmony, love and empathy.

The spiritual energy synthesis, thus, is caused by two kinds of opposing energies – hot and cold – manifested after combining the positive and the negative, similar but not completely analogous to yin and yang in the Buddhist tradition. By balancing two streams – Ida (mental) and Pingala (bodily) currents – the Susumna *nadi* (current of the Self) arises, leading to opening up of various *cakras* starting from the base of the spine and ending right above the head. This principle is called Nadi-Vigyan or Swar-Vigyan.

According to Ramdev, pranayama leads to a balance of the two energy streams and, thereby, to a complete manifestation of man as a spiritual entity. In Hatha Yoga, pranayama is the vital interface between the outward practices of the asanas and the inward surrendering yogic practices. It is a link between the mind and the body, and between the conscious and the unconscious. Practice of pranayama controls the mind and slows the breath, so that the prana or life force gets enhanced and deepened. This way, pranayama helps to connect the body to its battery, the solar plexus, where tremendous potential energy is stored. When tapped through specific techniques, this vital energy, or prana, is released for physical, mental and spiritual rejuvenation. The body cells start working in unison and bring back harmony and health to the system. Goraksa-Sataka also states that pranayama purifies vital life energy that flows through 72 lakh thousand two-hundred nerves and reaches Susumna so that man is relieved from all unhappiness and desires, and reaches a spiritually blissful state. Maharishi Patanjali also says that on acquiring proficiency in the four stages of pranayama, *citta* becomes free from ignorance, the mind is covered by the radiant light of knowledge of the ultimate reality, and the practitioner acquires fitness to reach the sixth stage of Yoga-Dharana (Yoga-Sutras, 2:51 and 2:53).

The key constituent of Ramdev's yoga doctrine, which differentiates his yoga from the classical yoga traditionally propounded by his predecessors as well as contemporaries, is the overbearing emphasis on pranayama. While the yoga traditions so far have focused on *yogasana*s, this technique was not given much importance. According to Ramdev, the purpose of asanas is to induce flexibility in the human body system, energize it, and, above all, bring in a balance. Asanas free the practitioner from *rajoguna* (body condition related to consumeristic and egostic lifestyle) by removing the distortions and disabilities of the physical body and inculcating a state of discipline in it. While pranayamas strengthen the software of the body, asanas empower its hardware.

In his method, the seer has also redesigned the conventional pranayama technique by introducing very rapid 'breathing in' and 'breathing out', to be sustained over a long duration. This way, he has brought a new dynamism to pranayama practice, making it a powerful work engine. With this method, he envisages benefits that are discrete and direct in the short term, accompanied by an immediate feeling of wellness as one enters into his yoga domain. Thus, Ramdev's pranayama is essentially built around a well-thought-out, result-oriented model, which offers people a quick remedy to gain good health through a comprehensive, easy-to-follow package of yogic practices demanding the least effort and time.

The Science of Pranayama

Ramdev's yoga doctrine delineates the meanings of prana and pranayama with respect to the physiological functioning of the human body.[2]

Vayu and Prana

According to Ramdev's doctrine, the human body is composed of five elements: *akasha* (space or vacuity), *vayu* (air), *agni* (fire), *jala* (water) and *prithvi* (earth). Of these five elements, *vayu* is said to be the essential element that keeps the body alive and maintains it. These five elements constitute three *dosha*s (humours) – *vata* (air), *pitta* (fire-heat; biles) and *kapha* (phlegm). The *pitta*, *kapha* and other constituents of the body, and the dross elements are all lame, as on their own they are not capable of going from one place to another or of affecting any function of the body. It is the *vayu* that takes them from one place to another, as the clouds in the sky drift from one place to another due to the force of wind. Besides, it is strong enough to analyse and separate the ingredients of various elements in the body including the dross element known as *mala* (excretions of the body like sweat, phlegm, urine, etc.).

Vayu when inspirited in the body by the process of breathing is called prana. It is felt and experienced in *vayu*, which is always in motion. It permeates the entire body and all its cells. The sense organs of the body take rest, as if in sleep or slumber, but prana always remains active. So long as the pranic energy continues functioning, the sentient beings remain alive. In the entire universe, this prana is the most potent and useful life-giving element. It is due to prana that all living things in the universe pulsate with life, and continue their communications and functions uninterruptedly, without the slightest pause. Prana provides us with vital energy which is the basis of our life. All the limbs, organs and important glands of the body, such as heart, lungs, brain and spinal cord, work with life energy by prana. This very energy makes our minds think and enables our alimentary system to digest and assimilate the food that we take, and also provides us immunity from various kinds of diseases. It is prana that is the cause of life and death. Life means to hold in or to be animated by prana, and death means to sever connection with prana.

Prana has five different nomenclatures, depending upon their locations and functions in the body. The generic prana is located in the area between the throat and the heart. It provides energy to the organs of breathing, organs of speech and oesophagus, and makes them active. *Apana* prana is located in the region between the navel (umbilicus), which is considered to be the centre and focal point of the organs of the body, and the toes of the feet. Its function is to cleanse the body of all the dross and used elements like excretions, sweat, phlegm, urine and faeces, and render the system clean. *Udana* prana is spread in the area between the throat and the head. It energizes the organs situated in the area. It covers organs such as eyes, ears, nostrils, and organs in the mouth, and lends lustre to the face. It activates pineal and pituitary glands as well.

Sumana prana is located in the region between the heart and the navel. It activates and controls the functioning of organs like liver, intestines, spleen and pancreas, as well as all the organs of the digestive system. *Vyana* prana is spread over the entire body. It energizes, controls and regulates the functioning of all the organs of the body, and synthesizes their functioning. In short, it activates all the organs of the body, its muscles, tissues, joints and *nadis* (arteries). There are also five sub-pranas known as *devadatta*, *naga*, *krinkal*, *kurma* and *dhananjay*, whose functions include sneezing, winking of the eyes, yawning, scratching the skin while itching, and hiccups. The functioning of all these pranas is primarily related to the subtle body (Pranamaya Kosh) known as etheric body.

The seer further states that all the sensory organs are full of faults because our eyes can see both good and bad scenes. The ears listen to both vulgar and decent language; similarly, the nose can smell both fragrance and odour, and the tongue can speak both lies and truth. The taste takes in both edible and inedible things; the good and bad thoughts arise in our mind. Therefore, nothing is perfect. Prana is completely faultless.

Therefore, we should take the shelter of the faultless prana in order to realize the faultless consciousness.

Pranayama: Regulating the Prana

According to the seer, prana means life force and *anayama* means control, and therefore, pranayama means mastering the life force within. Thus, control or regulation of prana is pranayama. Prana enters the body through nostrils. Respiration maintains life and is the basis of pranayama. It is through the control of respiration that the mind gets calm and peers into the inner world, and enables the practitioner to experience inner bliss. It has a powerful vitalizing effect on the body, mind and spirit. Prana is dissipated by stressful lifestyle and habits, as also by emotional outbursts, and this vital energy is constantly depleted and never recharged. Due to faulty lifestyle and unhealthy habits, we use only a fraction of our potential respiratory capacity. This results in fatigue caused by decrease in blood circulation and insufficient supply of oxygen to the blood cells. Quick, shallow breathing leads to oxygen starvation, which leads to reduced vitality, premature ageing, a poor immune system and fatigue.

Thus, pranayama is the very basis of the body and part of our natural self. It is just as natural as a newborn taking a deep breath immediately after birth, when his body starts moving. In the same way, we take deep breaths when we get tired after long hours of work. While the 'breathing in' technique rejuvenates the tissues of the body and supplies more oxygen to them, the 'breathing out' technique churns out the toxins from the body. Yet, doing pranayama does not mean only taking the air in the body (inhalation) and throwing it out (exhalation); along with oxygen, we also take in the vital energy into our body. This vital energy permeates the entire universe, and what we inhale and exhale is a fragment of it.

There are four stages in pranayama – to take the air in and retain it in the body for some time; to throw the air out; to keep the air out; and not allow the air to go in for the prescribed time. These four steps constitute one cycle of pranayama.

Benefits of Pranayama

Pranayama not only destroys the bodily and mental abnormalities, but also frees the mind from untruthfulness, ignorance and all other painful and unpleasant experiences of the body and mind. It influences the subtle and the physical bodies in a greater measure than *yogasana*s do, and that too in a perceptible manner. Physically, pranayama appears to be a systematic exercise of respiration, which makes the lungs stronger, improves blood circulation, makes a man healthier, and bestows upon him the boon of a long life.

From physiology, we know that the air (prana) we breathe in fills our lungs and spreads across the entire body, providing it with essential food and oxygen. Not only that, the veins also collect the dross elements from the body and take them to the heart and then to the lungs, which throw the useless materials like carbon dioxide out of the body through the act of exhalation. If this action of the respiratory system is done regularly and efficiently, lungs become stronger and blood becomes pure.

However, most people do not have the habit of breathing deeply, with the result that only one-fourth part of the lungs is brought into action. Like the honeycomb, lungs are made of about 73 million cells, comparable to a sponge. On normal breathing, to which we all are accustomed, only about 23 million pores in the lungs get oxygen, whereas the remaining 50 million pores remain deprived of this benefit, with the result that they get contaminated by diseases like tuberculosis and respiratory diseases like cough and bronchitis. As a consequence, blood circulation gets affected and heart becomes weak, leading to an early death. Further, mental diseases like excitement, anxiety, fear, anger, disappointment and lust for sex can be calmed down by regular practice of pranayama. This practice also improves the functions of the brain cells, leading to improvement in memory and the faculty of discrimination and observation.

According to medical science, nature determines lifespan on the basis of the respiratory capacity. The life span of animals depends on the number of respirations. For example, the tortoise, whose rate of respiration per minute is about five breaths, lives for about 400 years, establishing the fact that the lesser the speed of respiration per minute, the longer the lifespan. A man who regularly performs pranayama needs to take a lesser number of breaths and therefore lives longer.

The Pranayama Package

Ramdev's yoga doctrine is built around a well-researched pranayama package consisting of seven key pranayamas to be practised in a sequence. These are: Kapalbhaati, Anulom-Vilom, Bhastrika, Brahmri, Udgeeth, Pranav and Bahaya.

In Kapalbhaati Pranayama, the breaths are exhaled at a fast pace so that the polluted air within the body is thrown out and the blood is enriched with oxygen, leading to strengthening of the prana. Pranayama exerts pressure on all the organs of the abdominal cavity and the vibration in the intestines cures constipation and piles, while the quick movement of air clears the blockage of arteries and cleans the lungs.

In Anulom-Vilom, the alternative nostril breathing requires inhaling from left nostril and exhaling from right nostril, and vice-versa, leading to balancing of the respiratory system and changing of the whole biochemistry. This classical pranayama cures eye-, nose- and ear-related problems. The blood pressure becomes normal; eyesight is improved; white or black cataract is cured; the enlarged bone of the ear is corrected automatically; and is extremely helpful in curing brain-related diseases. The quantity of oxygen in lungs purifies the blood and improves the circulation. This in turn cures ringworm, eczema and itching white and dark patches on the skin. The complexion also becomes fair.

Bhastrika Pranayama improves and strengthens the function of the heart, activates the inactive body, and improves the function of the respiratory system. Udgeeth Pranayama, similar to the Buddhist practice, leads to a journey within, aided by breathing and sound as the vehicle. The breathing is kept so low that even a piece of cotton kept in front of the nose should not move. As one experiences the breath from within, he feels it at the tip of the nose, but slowly it will be experienced deep within, leading to the stage of deep meditation. This pranayama helps in getting sound sleep and in getting rid of bad dreams.

In Brahmri Pranayama, the practitioner breathes in till the lungs are full of air. The ears are now closed with both the thumbs, and the eyes with the middle fingers of hands on respective sides with little pressure. The forehead is pressed with both the index fingers lightly. After closing both the eyes, the nose bridge is pressed from the sides with the remaining fingers. He now concentrates his mind on Ajna Cakra (between eyebrows). He exhales slowly, making a buzzing sound like that of a bee. This practice makes the mind steady and is beneficial in conditions of mental tension and agitation, high blood pressure and heart diseases.

Pranav Pranayama, hailed by Patanjali as *tatra pratyayaikataanataa dhyaanam*, is the highest stage of pranayama, the true stage of dhyana (concentration). Dhyana is associated with us every moment and with every work of life, and in its absence, success in attaining any material or spiritual goal is not possible. This pranayama leads to control of the mind and sensory organs, and the practitioner gets into deep concentration and attains priceless bliss suitable for meditation. Internal negative energy gets transformed into positive energy, and as life is filled up with positive energy, one attains chastity and good health. It is to be practised with every breath so softly that its sound should not be heard even by the practitioner.

Bahaya Pranayama is practised by sitting in Padmasana or Siddhasana. The practitioner first breathes out as much as possible and then enters into Mula Bandha, Uddiyana Bandha and Jalandhara Bandha simultaneously, keeping the breath out. He then breathes in slowly, simultaneously unlocking all the *bandha*s, and starts breathing normally without retaining the breath in. This pranayama helps in controlling fluctuations of the mind, improves digestion, is beneficial in curing all kinds of abdominal ailments, sharpens intelligence, cleanses the entire body, causes the semen to rise up, and cures all kinds of abnormalities.

The practice of these seven pranayamas takes around 45 minutes. In case of any disease, a specific asana can be added. The pace should be slow or medium depending on the condition of the body.

Supplementary Pranayamas

In addition to the above basic pranayamas, Ramdev also suggests a package of six supplementary pranayamas in order to enhance the overall benefits. These are: Surya Bhedi Pranayama, Chandra Bhedi Pranayama, Ujjayi Pranayama, Karna Rogantak Pranayama, Shitali Pranayama, Sitkari Pranayama and Nadi Shodhan Pranayama.

Surya Bhedi Pranayama is performed through *pooraka* (inhalation) with right nostril and *kumbhaka* (filling up with air) with Jalandhara and Mula Bandha, following it with *rechak* (exhalation) with left nostril. While doing *kumbhaka*, the focus should be on the brightness of the Sun. This pranayama controls ageing, improves heart function, reduces weight and cures diseases caused due to *vata* and *kapha*, blood impurities, skin problems, stomach worms, leprosy, syphilis, contagious diseases, indigestion and gynaecological problems. Chandra Bhedi Pranayama, which is opposite to the Surya Bhedi version, is performed through *pooraka* with left nostril and then *antar-kumbhaka* (shorter retention), followed by *rechak* with right nostril. While doing *kumbhaka*, one should think about the shining Moon. This pranayama brings down the body temperature, helps to overcome fatigue and decreases heartbeat. It also controls the anxiety and the burning sensation caused due to *pitta*.

In Ujjayi Pranayama, inhaling is done by contracting the throat, resulting in a sound similar to snoring. It cures chronic cold, cough, dysentery, indigestion, liver problem, phlegm, fever and spleen; makes the voice sweet and melodious; and cures lisping in children. In Karna Rogantak Pranayama, *pooraka* is done with both the nostrils, and then the mouth and nostrils are closed and the *pooraka* air is thrown out from both the ears. It is beneficial for curing ear diseases and improves hearing power. Shitali Pranayama is performed by folding the tongue and doing *pooraka* with mouth by inhaling from tongue, thereby filling up air in lungs. It is beneficial in curing diseases related to tongue, mouth and throat, as also in the diseases of spleen, fever and indigestion. The practitioner is able to control thirst and hunger with regular practice. It controls high blood pressure and is beneficial in curing *pitta*-related diseases, and also purifies the blood.

In Sitkari Pranayama, the tongue is twined upwards and the upper and lower rows of teeth are joined, while the lips are kept open, inhaling from mouth until air fills up the lungs. It cures dental problems like pyorrhoea as well as diseases of throat, mouth, nose and tongue. It helps in curtailing the requirement for sleep and controls the body temperature. Patients of high blood pressure should practise it 50 to 60 times. In Nadi Shodhan Pranayama, the breath is stopped after inhaling from left nostril, and Mula Bandha and Jalandhara Bandha are entered. Jalandhara Bandha is then removed and exhalation is done slowly with right nostril. After exhaling completely, inhaling is done with right nostril and *kumbhaka* is performed; the breath is controlled followed by inside exhalation from left nostril at slow pace. This helps in concentrating the mind on the prana and the mind becomes stable. In Nadi Shodhan Pranayama, the ratio of *pooraka, antar-kumbhaka* and *rechak* is kept as 1:2:2. It is performed at a very slow pace. The benefits are similar to those of Anulom-Vilom Pranayama.

Orthodox Yoga Schools and Ramdev's 'Method'

Before Ramdev's arrival, yoga courses were offered mostly by well-marked institutions in the country and also by their highly publicized branches/centres abroad with a comparatively narrow mass base. These institutions catered largely to the elite and other well-to-do seekers (of course, against a huge fee). They offered refuge to a big chunk of foreign clientele determined to rediscover themselves and their health by experimenting with an oriental therapy.

In contrast, Ramdev – perhaps because of his humble background – has triggered a sea change in the social perceptions of, and accessibility to, yoga. He has virtually declassed the very system of yoga education, bringing it to the doorsteps of the common man and within the precincts of a highly successful collective endeavour. In this way, he has freed yoga from its ivory-tower trappings, defying along the way the gross commodification of this sacred discipline. Ramdev has, thus, emerged as a liberator of yoga itself.

The Individual's Emancipation through Yoga

Apart from the yoga-and-health synthesis, Ramdev's doctrine also lays the path for an individual's emancipation. It postulates one's true self-realization or virtually a 'rebirthing' through the Noble Truth of yoga. According to him, 'To become free from sorrow and the causes of sorrow such as disease, fear, sadness, birth and death is salvation. That with which man crosses the ocean of sorrow is called pilgrimage. You will not die, fear not. He, who fears dies. He, who does not fear, does not die. Thus, just as a sculptor makes stone idols, we too sculpt our own destinies.'

Ramdev considers expectations, ignorance and ego as the causes of unhappiness. Everyone wishes to be happy all the time, but keeps on running behind comforts and luxuries. Fire increases when we add clarified butter or oil; similarly, luxuries and comforts increase desires. Man remains unhappy due to these increasing desires and aspirations. He says, 'Creation is limitation; the child has limitations when it [is] in the mother's womb but it progresses. Therefore, we all should learn to live in limitations and fulfil our duties and responsibilities with all sincerity and dedication. This is because yoga does not mean moving away from responsibilities but is to realize and fulfil them. Yoga makes one more competitive and capable of reaching the goals. It appears as if the whole horizon is open in front of him.'

He further states, 'An individual's personality and stature is as big as the universe, but along with that it should also be cold like water, huge like the sky, tolerant like the earth, and speedy like the wind. A man faces different types of obstacles, challenges, defeat, defame in his life, which should be faced with tolerance, courage, bravery and valour. Lust kills the love within us. Therefore, a person should try to avoid it and practice pure love. Love, service, respect, dedication, equality, politeness, duty, respect and faith are the basis of happiness. Passion, ignorance, desires, unhappiness and other negative thoughts are removed and soul gets the ultimate happiness, brightness and a peaceful abode.'

Salvation or freedom, therefore, is possible only by parting ways with ignorance, the seer says. Any person can achieve emancipation, as he did, if he makes use of his inner valour and the conviction to seek the Truth. He says, 'Have faith in your own intellect and understanding, and become a self-dependent seeker, autonomous in the domain of reason and reality and completely qualified with a vision that has been built on the evidence and experience of yoga. One can experiment, observe and logically verify with his own experiences the power of yoga – the righteous way of life – in changing his thoughts and actions.'

Ramdev further elaborates upon the spiritual requirements necessary to achieve salvation. To reach this state, a seeker needs to establish control over five states with practice and asceticism – evidence (*pramana*), hostility (*viparya*), variation (*vikalpa*), sleep (*nidra*) and memory (*smriti*). That which is known through the sense organs and the mind perceives – knowledge of fire after seeing smoke, etc. – is assumption; those that have similar forms are known through comparison, such as comparing a cow with a nilgai. The thing that has evidence, reasoning and order of creation is called 'possible'. The knowledge that is based on absence is called 'absence'. Thus, when someone tells another to bring water, the person who is bringing the water sees that water is not here but is to be got from where it is. This knowledge is called 'absence' evidence. Therefore, the true advices or views of completely reliable, godlike men are called 'word' or evidence. The history that is based on such 'word' evidence and a path free from untruth is called traditional theory.[3]

Further, he says, our outer-world perceptions are governed by what is called in the scriptures as *mithyagryanam: ataroopapratishtham*, which is established in the form of a thing as a collection of myths. This is transpiration (*viprayay*), that is, it is not established in the real form of a thing because it is not obtained in the same form as is considered to be in the related object. For instance, we see a rope in the dark and think it to be a snake. This is myth because when we see it in light, then the rope will not have the qualities and features of a snake. Hence, we see that the knowledge obtained in the form of snake is not established in the form of rope. Therefore, a seeker should not go for what is easily perceived but seek to outdo the myths surrounding ideas and things, and get a grip of the true reality for his final release to freedom.

Vikalpa (variation) is about developing an understanding of and control over the ever-varying nature of mind. The condition of the mind which gives us the knowledge of dream and reality is called sleep. During *nidra* (sleep), the *tama* quality is predominant and subsides the *raja* and *satva* qualities. Hence, *tama* is more active during sleep and we feel the deficiency or lack of something in our mind. The outward perceptions and their transposition, and the sleep conditions of the mind give us the experience of things, events and persons. While we are asleep or awake, the impressions of those experiences are imprinted in our mind. *Smriti* (memory) is the remembrance of past experiences with respect to the values stored in our mind. These values are with respect to the experience, and memory is with respect to the values. Memory also has values and the values again generate memories. A yogi in his emancipated state overcomes the values and experiences attached to memory.

Finally, when a practitioner of yoga gets control over the above-mentioned states, his life becomes blissful, and as the seer observes, 'There is a smile on his or her face and there is natural shine. There is sweetness in his speech, he always speaks the truth, he is empathetic, and he has love and likes to help others.'

Sukkha: Total Happiness through Linking One's Salvation to Energizing a Collective Way of Life

Energizing a collective way of life is one of the most productive elements of Ramdev's doctrine as it lays the path for grassroots activism. According to the seer, reaching a state of yoga consciousness is not enough; it is necessary to direct it towards energizing collective consciousness. Yoga is not for one's own salvation only, but for others' salvation as well. It facilitates leading a collective, and not an individual way of life. It is internal consciousness, which transforms us internally and externally. Its realization with focused energy and a sense of compassion towards all living beings is the key to one's total happiness. But compassion is not sufficient. It is in the contemplation and manifestation of compassion in real action that we live a fruitful life.

Thus, Ramdev's doctrine is a powerful rendering on a spiritual, emancipated man living life in complete happiness and bliss, dedicating his newfound enlightenment in the service of society. As he says, the aim of life is not worldly pleasures, gambling, consuming alcohol and meat, travel, leisure and entertainment. Life is the ability to give satisfaction, happiness and contentment to others with service, and obtaining contentment, happiness and complete satisfaction with devotion. Yet, spiritual presence does not mean passively tolerating crime, atrocities and injustice, as it is a bigger crime when compared to doing it, says the master.

Ramdev, in pronouncing the social role of enlightenment, has reaffirmed similar views of our past spiritual masters. Swami Vivekananda, the upholder of the principle of *atmano mokshartham jagat-hitaya cha* (for one's own salvation and for the welfare of the World), held that even the desire for personal salvation has to be given up, and only tireless work for the salvation of others is the true mark of the enlightened person. He said, 'So long as the millions live in hunger and ignorance, I hold every man a traitor who, having been educated at their expense, pays not the least heed to them.' He further said, 'If you want any good to come, flung all those bells and other junk, and worship every human being who is embodiment of God. The living gods are dying without food and education. Our country is sick; it is a madhouse everywhere. I salute those of you who have a little brain and I urge them to spread [like] wildfire.'[4]

In the ten principles of the Arya Samaj, Swami Dayananda also enshrined the idea that 'all actions should be performed with the prime objective of benefiting mankind'. For him, moksha is a lower calling (due to its benefit to one individual) than the calling to emancipate others.[5] Swami Sahajanand Saraswati had said, 'As religious robes had long exploited the peasants, now he would exploit those robes on behalf of the peasants.' When landlords raised the question as to how a sanyasi (mendicant) was taking part in the temporal problems of the poor, Sahajanand quoted the scriptures: 'Mendicants are selfish, living away from society; they try for their own salvation without caring for others. I cannot do that; I do not want my own salvation apart from that of the many destitute. I will stay with them, live with them and die with them.'[6]

Secularizing Yoga beyond Religions and Cultures

In the domain of yoga and spiritualism, Ramdev has emerged as the first spiritual leader in our times who seeks to present yoga beyond the pale of any religious connotations. According to Ramdev, 'Yoga is not [a] method of worship but it is a live science and a complete system of education. It has nothing to do with religion. It is not Hinduism. It is for all people, whether he be Hindu, Muslim or Christian. One can say "Om" when he is doing yoga. Another can pronounce "Allah-u-Akbar" or the name of Jesus. It was science that discovered electricity and put together airplanes. They are not for any one group of people. It is for all people of the world irrespective of their religious beliefs. Likewise, yoga is also for all. Any person who practises it, gets free from any community or sect or religion affinities, remains free from prejudices and moves closer to the Truth.'[7] Significantly, in Hatha-yoga-pradipika, Swami Swatamarama proclaimed that worship of the Gods is not more than a secondary means to reach out to the Higher Being or the self-realized and blissful Self, indicating that Hatha Yoga philosophy, since its inception, has remained spiritually unique as it transcends the boundaries of any one religion or cult. Sri Tirumalai Krishnamacharya and his camp followers, B. K. S. Iyengar and K. Pattabhi Jois, also upheld the secular vision of yoga.

Yoga beyond Patenting and Copyright

Amidst the current tendencies the world over to patent each and every element of knowledge, Ramdev is against the recent attempts of patenting some yoga forms. As the global patent regime is ruthlessly taking over indigenous knowledge as seen in the two recent applications filed in the United States for patenting yoga, the seer and several other yoga enthusiasts and experts have strongly opposed the attempt to patent yoga overseas. According to them, patenting of any kind is highly unjustified and when it comes to patenting yoga, it is even more criminal. Patenting an invention is understood but trying to patent organic matter like turmeric and neem and then knowledge like that of yoga is very unfortunate. If the copying of western drugs is illegal, so is the patenting of yoga.[8] The seer said, 'Yoga being a universal knowledge system cannot be patented. Nobody can claim ownership for it; it is for all the people to use. Yoga can't be owned and run like a company. Even other medicines should not be patented. When you patent something, the price goes up. Life of all is equally important. The ordinary sick man is unable to purchase the lifesaving medicines because they are highly priced.'

Towards Reinstating the Yoga–Ayurveda Combine

Apart from yoga, Ramdev has taken up the task of establishing Ayurveda as a competing alternative to modern medicine. According to him, *Ayurveda and yoga have remained mostly neglected in the free Indian nation, and hardly anything constructive has been done to make progress in these fields.* He has taken up a comprehensive appraisal of the ancient medical works for developing a new set of medicines in the scientific way for virtually every form of disease.

Institutional Legacy

Ramdev has, with much enthusiasm and mind-boggling speed, built an impressive institutional infrastructure dedicated to the cause of yoga.[9] These include Patanjali Yogpeeth, Divya Yog Mandir Trust and Patanjali Yog University, all in Haridwar; Vidhyateertha Gurukul, a residential school for children in Haryana; and Yoga Gram, a health resort in Haridwar. He also launched a medicinal plants research programme to promote research on extinct and new medicinal plants and their medicinal applications.

Divya Yog Mandir Trust

In 1995, Ramdev, in association with Acharya Karamveer and Acharya Balkrishna, set up the Divya Yog Mandir Trust, a yoga school-cum-therapy centre, at the Kripalu Bagh Ashram, with the aim of imparting yoga training to the people. They set the mission statement of the trust as:

> To establish a learning centre wherein it will be the prime objective to foster education based on modern scientific learning; to promote a healthy mind and a vibrant body enabling facilitation of spiritual development to rejuvenate latent noble virtues in children so that their lives epitomize the values of beauty, dedication, and rationalism, thereby engendering a world of harmony, friendship, brotherhood, peace, and prosperity.

Patanjali Yogpeeth and Patanjali Yog University

In 2006, Ramdev set up the sprawling Patanjali Yogpeeth and Patanjali Yog University outside Haridwar for promoting advanced research in traditional systems of medicine and yoga. The Yogpeeth, a multi-million-rupee venture spread over 100 acres, is the seer's dream project. Conceived as a rival to the World Health Organization, this institution is set to become the world's largest centre for yoga and Ayurveda with world-class facilities for treatment, research and a university. On completion, the Yogpeeth will become the world's largest hospital treating 5,000 patients a day. It will have a residential complex for 1,000 patients and a hall for 5,000 people to practise yoga. A top-class Ayurvedic college and a Panchkarma Institute are also on the anvil. The Yogpeeth is now engaged in developing productive linkages with various medical institutions in an effort to study and improve yoga's effectiveness in the cure and management of a large number of diseases. Patanjali Yogpeeth already has a network of more than 500 centres across the country.

Brahmakalp Dispensary

Brahmakalp Dispensary is the flagship institution of the trust to build a nationwide network of Ayurvedic treatment and research centres. It is equipped with sophisticated gadgets. At present, 40 doctors in the dispensary's OPD offer treatment to nearly 2,000 people everyday. Some days, the dispensary sells medicines worth Rs. 3,000 a minute. Free treatment is for poor patients. In a bid to promote Ayurveda, Divya Yog Trust has tied up with about 600 qualified Ayurvedic practitioners who are offering treatment for a variety of diseases, some of them termed 'incurable' by the modern system. The number of such centres is around 500. Acharya Balkrishna heads the Brahmakalp Dispensary. He had completed his education in Sampooranand Sanskrit University and Acharya Baldev's Gurukul Kalva in Haryana.

Medicinal Plants Research Programme

The trust's laboratory conducts research on extinct and new medicinal plants. For several years, four medicinal plants of Ashtavarga were considered to be extinct due to natural reasons. However, the trust's researchers have found the plants in the snow-laden peaks of the Himalayas. The laboratory scientists are also working on the preservation and medical use of several other medicinal plants. The trust has published monograms *Divya Aushadhiya Sungandhit evam Soundaryakaran poudh*, *Aushadh Darshan* and *Medicinal Plants of Ashtavarga*, which contain the introduction to medicinal plants, their qualities and benefits. Patanjali Yogpeeth is also setting up a herbal research centre this year.

The *Gurukul* Network

The Divya Yog Trust has built several *gurukuls* (residential schools) with the aim of providing a combination of modern and traditional knowledge for the all-round mental and physical development of students.

Village-level Master Yoga Trainers

The seer claims to have trained about 35,000 persons, who are now well-equipped to hold yoga classes in different parts of the country. In the first phase of the next five years, his target is to train one lakh instructors who will be able to impart yoga training to one crore people, so that they stay away from diseases and avoidable medication through practice of yoga. By the end of this decade, he plans to take yoga to all the approximately six lakh villages in the country. The guru's ultimate goal is to take yoga to every corner of the world.

Yoga Gram

The Divya Trust has recently established this facility in Haridwar as a health resort. Located in a forest area, it was built within a period of 70 days.

Media Hero's Nationwide Yoga Movement

Baba Ramdev, within a span of less than five years, has unleashed a mass yoga movement in the country. The yoga treatment camps have assured direct benefits to more than 50 lakh people, with attendance at one camp often being as high as 20,000. Ramdev's pranayama techniques — Kapalbhaati, Anulom-Vilom and Bhastrika — have become massively popular. Among his celebrated yoga camps are those at Rashtrapati Bhavan, which is the residence of the president of India, and at the House of Commons in London, UK. At present, the penetration of Ramdev's yoga movement is rather weak in the southern states of Tamil Nadu, Kerala, Karnataka and Andhra Pradesh.

With his popular yoga discourses on television, Ramdev has emerged as a highly respected media icon. The seer plunged into the Indian media when Sanskar (television channel) started airing his yogic classes. Overnight, he became a sensation and soon he moved to Aastha (another televison channel), where his show set record as one of the biggest draws ever in the history of Indian television. Statistics show that over 85 million people follow his yoga camps via TV channels. Today, his TV programmes are telecast in nearly 170 countries spread over Africa, Australia, Asia, Europe and America. He has launched a large package of CDs/DVDs and books on yoga, pranayama and herbal remedies, and also a research-oriented monthly magazine, *Yog Sandesh*, on yoga, spiritualism, Ayurveda and culture. The magazine is being published in 11 Indian languages without any source of revenue through advertisements.

While Ramdev is very critical of the onslaught of modern scientific knowledge and technology, his skills in management of communication and media technologies leave even seasoned media campaigners envious. The way he has made use of TV and CD packages as well as the Internet shows his immense ability to subordinate alien technology-driven products and practices with the ease of a thorough professional. His live yoga demos look like a medical science-lab class, which are replicated by his media-activated disciples at homes, parks and camps. In fact, this TV lab-to-field teaching–learning mode is the most distinguished feature of his yoga education programme.

According to media researchers, the phenomenal success of the seer's marketing strategy is built around mass customization, wherein the requirements of customers are catered to without delay.[10] In a very meticulous manner, he has tickled the pulse of the people in search of a healthy lifestyle, and has managed to fine-tune his package to suit the needs of all. Baba Ramdev's media campaigns, in fact, address the three value aspects of mass customization. His 'product leadership discipline' has created the 'best product' value proposition, that is, his products have the greatest performance impact for its customers. The 'operational excellence discipline' has provided virtually no-cost services with high product reliability and ease of distribution. The 'customer familiarity discipline' built by the seer's organizations has developed the 'best total solution' scheme in terms of identifying exact problems of the customers, providing the best solutions, and taking charge of implementing the same.

Ramdev's unique blend of yoga and Ayurveda reflects extremely high value addition to these ancient systems. The service that is being provided by Baba Ramdev is well orchestrated with the desired service expectations, so that his followers eventually become the brand evangelists. It has set the product and the producer of that product apart from the competition. This way, Baba Ramdev has proven a new media outreach methodology of 'advertising and at the same time not advertising'. He proves the dictum of mass customization – *Aham Brahamasmi*, meaning that I am omnipresent and omnipotent. But the seer does not want his method to be called branding or corporatization of yoga; he is merely promoting it as a way of life.

Ramdev's Personal Values and Lifestyle

As already said, Ramdev never talks about his family or in terms of 'my home' because this is the cause of attachment. Yet, he is against the culture of the sanyasis. According to him, a sanyasi must maintain a relation between his internal and external personality, and work in the interests of society. Sanyas is a mental condition wherein one is free of worldly things, desires and aspirations, but it does not mean that one is all alone. He wishes to be associated with the entire mankind, rather than being the pride of a community.

The master also asserts that he is no more than a humble teacher in yellow robes; it is perchance that he has been destined to be a means for change in human thinking and actions, waiting to unfold a new meaning and understanding of human purpose and the world. He asks his disciples to desist from making claims – as done by many others – about the psychic powers and exhibition of extraordinary deeds. The seer does not wish to be ever idolized or worshipped. He is vehemently against the guru/godman culture spreading rapidly, particularly through TV channels. When his followers tell him that they want to install his pictures at their homes, Ramdev makes a sarcastic remark – 'Why mine? Adorn your house with the pictures of your parents and of your motherland, which will inspire you to become a good human being!'

The sage follows a stringent daily schedule. He gets up in the wee hours of the morning at 3 a.m. and then does pranayama for over an hour. By 5 a.m. he is at the yoga camp. After the camp, between 7:30 and 8:30 a.m. he again devotes time to yoga. During the day, he spends time in meeting people, writing and, of course, practising yoga and pranayama. He goes to bed by 10 p.m. and apart from the five hours of sleep, does not sleep at all during the day. His diet consists of fruits, dry fruits, some green vegetables and milk.

Notes and References

1. For information on Ramdev's early life and his views on his yoga-healing method and its benefits are taken from the following sources: *Yog Sandesh*, (January) Divya Mandir Trust, Haridwar, 2006; *Yog Sandesh*, (August) Divya Mandir Trust, Haridwar, 2008; *Yog Sandesh*, (March) Divya Mandir Trust, Haridwar, 2009; Swami Ramdev, *Jeevan Darshan* (The Philosophy of Life), in Hindi, Divya Mandir Trust, Haridwar, 2008; 'Swami Ramdev Maharaj', http://knowyoga.org/tiki-index.php?page=Swami%20Ramdev&redirectpage=Ramdev

2. Swami Ramdev, *Pranayama: Its Philosophy and Practice*, Divya Mandir Trust, Haridwar, 2004.

3. Swami Ramdev, 'The Stages of Deep Meditation', *Yog Sandesh*, (January) Divya Mandir Trust, Haridwar, 2006, p. 39.

4. Swami Vivekananda, *Complete Works of Swami Vivekananda*, Volume I, Advaita Ashrama, Mayavati, Almora, 2001; Arun Kumar Biswas, *Swami Vivekananda and the Indian Quest for Socialism*, Firma KLM Private Ltd, Calcutta, 1986; Narasingha Sil, *Swami Vivekananda: A Reassessment*, Susquehanna Univeristy Press, Selinsgrove, 1997.

5. Swami Dayanand, *Satyarath Prakash*, Arya Pratinidhi Sabha, New Delhi, 1984; Arvind Sharma, *Modern Hindu Thought*, Oxford University Press, New Delhi, 2002.

6. Swami Sahajanand, *Mera Jeewan Sangharsha* (My Life Struggle), Peoples' Publication House, New Delhi, 1952.

7. Swami Ramdev, 'Golden Words of Swami Ramdev', *Yog Sandesh*, (January) Divya Mandir Trust, Haridwar, 2006; Swami Ramdev, *Jeevan Darshan* (The Philosophy of Life), in Hindi, Divya Mandir Trust, Haridwar, 2008.

8. 'Yoga Enthusiasts Oppose Patenting Yoga Overseas', www.bio-medicine.org/medicine-news/Yoga-Enthusiasts-Oppose-Patenting-Yoga-Overseas-21668-1/.

9. Swami Ramdev, 2005, op. cit.; *Yog Sandesh*, (January) Divya Mandir Trust, Haridwar, 2006.

10. Mrinalini Pandey, 'Mass Customization: The Success Story of Baba Ramdev', www.indianmba.com/Faculty_Column/FC851/fc851.html.

Chapter 4

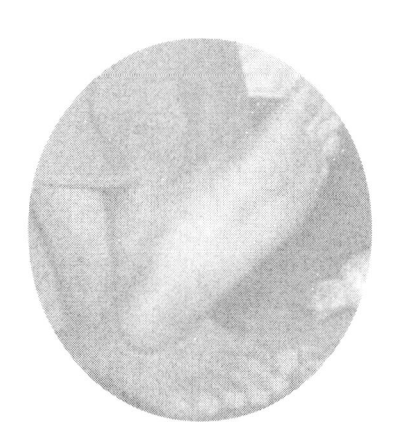

ESTABLISHING MEDICAL EFFICACY
OF YOGA

व्यक्ति नहीं
व्यक्तित्व की पूजा करें

... the seer stresses that yoga and alternative medical systems should be viewed as the actual modern medical science. Yoga, Ayurveda and other indigenous medicine regimes should be promoted as the mainstream medical systems, and these should be the main focus of medical research in the country and elsewhere, using modern clinical diagnosis techniques and equipment.

The wide appreciation of Ramdev's yoga can be attributed to the growing volume and complexity of illnesses in today's world. This sickness syndrome is being caused primarily by a stressful life in which the anxieties and tensions are sought to be vented through indulgence in pleasures both of mind and body. In the Buddhist viewpoint, this indulgence itself leads to a furthering of desire for more gratification so that one is trapped in the vicious circle of *trishna*. Thus, an ever-growing materialism is leading to an unbearable demand to prove oneself materially successful and ensure survival in a highly competitive milieu. As the sickness grip gets tightened, it creates a never-ceasing need for a vast variety of treatments, which in turn perpetuates an ever-expanding drug regimen to address the complexities of diseases. But this drug-held society, the curse of modern ways of life, is rendered perpetually sick not only of the diseases themselves but also of the clinical, symptom-based treatments. The end result is unbearable unhappiness and trauma in which both mind and body suffer. An acute desperation develops and the sufferers now start experimenting with whatever treatment is available.

According to Ramdev, the main beneficiary of the complex disease syndrome is the mainstream medical sector, which has become big business as seen in its growing commercialization. The business of medicines is the second biggest challenge in the world of lethal weapons.

Doctors, big hospitals, pharmaceutical companies and traders depend on the cycle of more people becoming ill. The pharmaceutical market is promoted through many unethical and profit-oriented strategies, wherein 60 to 70 per cent medicines are priced 100 to 10,000 times more than their manufacturing costs. Despite spending almost 6,00,000 crore of rupees on health services, only 35 per cent of people are able to afford modern medical treatment, while the rest 65 per cent are not even capable of availing allopathic treatment. Quoting the WHO report of 2005–06, Ramdev informs that around 4,89,520 crore of rupees are being spent on health services annually in the country. If we aim to provide health services to the entire population, we require a whopping 11,35,700 crore of rupees.[1]

Ramdev in his call has asked people to come out of the overpowering and alienating complexities of modern treatment. He wants to reinstall the philanthropic aspects of health care and provide easy accessibility for the poor in terms of low-cost, patient-friendly solutions and establishing confidence building between the healer and the healed. In this way, the seer stresses that yoga and alternative medical systems should be viewed as the actual modern medical science. Yoga, Ayurveda and other indigenous medicine regimes should be promoted as the mainstream medical systems, and these should be the main focus of medical research in the country and elsewhere, using modern clinical diagnosis techniques and equipment.

The Clinical Trials

After mobilizing thousands of people and garnering mass acceptance of his healing method, Ramdev took a highly ambitious initiative to establish the efficacy of his method by moving into the very arena of modern medicine. He set up an elaborate system of clinical trials to quantify the impact of his method on the human body by borrowing freely from the established norms and practices of clinical studies in modern medical science. For this purpose, a panel of senior allopathic doctors was set up to conduct the clinical tests. Five such studies and a large-size survey have been reported.[2]

The First Three Foundation Studies

Three short-term clinical studies were undertaken in 2005 and 2006 at the residential yoga camps to examine the efficacy of Ramdev's yoga and pranayama package. The salient features of these studies and their clinical results are discussed below.

Profile of Studies

Study I (2005): This study was held during six residential camps of seven-day duration, organized in 2005 with a large sample of patients. The study was divided into six sub-categories to evaluate the impact of yoga on respiratory diseases, diabetes management, obesity and kidney diseases. For respiratory sub-study, the sample size was of 10,000 patients who were tested for pulmonary function (PFT) before and after the camps. The participants were made to practise yoga and pranayama for two hours in the morning and evening. They did Bhastrika,

Kapalbhaati, Bahaya, Anulom-Vilom, Brahmri, Udgeeth, Ujjayi and some asanas.

For blood profile, 1,044 patients were tested for ECG (electrocardiogram) and complete lipid profile was prepared before and after the camps in order to examine the effect of pranayama. The tests included total cholesterol, LDL (low-density lipoprotein) cholesterol, HDL (high-density lipoprotein) cholesterol, VLDL (very-low-density lipoprotein) cholesterol and triglycerides. The patients were also tested for blood pressure before and after the camps. Regular practice of pranayama and Shavasana was held.

For endocrine glands (internal secretion glands and related diseases), the patients practised Ujjayi Pranayama along with deep and mild *kumbhaka*. The thyroid hormones are helpful in oxidation that takes place in bones, flesh, brain and other organs. They help burning of glucose in body organs, production of glucose from glycogen in liver, digestion of fat and cholesterol in blood, digestion of proteins in body, evacuation of nitrogen and phosphorus, and take care of heart functions. Hyperthyroidism leads to lean body, fast heartbeats, and tremors, whereas hypothyroidism causes swelling of the body, increases cholesterol level and affects metabolism in the body. In the study, the participants underwent thyroid function test (T_3 – Triiodothyronine, T_4 – Thyroxine and TSH – thyroid-stimulating hormone) before and after the camp. For diabetes patients, the practice of Kapalbhaati, Bhastrika, Mandookasan, Yoga Mudrasan and other asanas was taken up. They were tested for blood-sugar level before and after the camp. Tables 1 to 5 present the overall results of this study.

Study 2 (2006): This investigation was held during two residential yoga camps to study the effects of yoga and pranayama on obesity, high blood pressure, respiratory disorder, heart disease, thyroid dysfunction (hypo- and hyperthyroidism), diabetes, liver disorder, kidney disorder, arthritis and cancer. In the case of obese patients, the weight and lipid profile were measured before and after the camp. The patients of high blood pressure and heart disease were tested for lipid profile and electrocardiogram was conducted. Diabetes patients underwent fasting for blood-sugar test. The patients of respiratory diseases underwent pulmonary function test, while thyroid function test (T_3, T_4 and TSH) was done for thyroid patients. Haemoglobin test was done for patients of anaemia.

Patients with liver disorder were tested for liver function, and kidney patients were tested for kidney function (serum creatinine, serum urea and haemoglobin level). The cancer patients were tested for AFP (alpha-fetoprotein), PSA (prostate specific antigen) and CA-125 (a protein found in ovarian cancer cells). For arthritis patients, measurements of RA factor (Rheumatoid factor used for the diagnosis of rheumatoid arthritis), uric acid and haemoglobin were carried out. The patients were given simple and light food during the medical tests. The patients practised yoga and pranayama for two hours in the morning and evening. They were not allowed to take any medicine during the medical test.

Study 3 (2006): This investigation was focused on studying the impact of yoga on bone mineral density. It involved 128 patients, of whom 50 patients (18 male and 32 female) of osteoporosis and 78 patients (43 male and 35 female) of osteopenia were selected. Only non-yoga practitioners were selected for this purpose. The patients underwent a package of seven asanas and pranayama. During yoga practice, the patients were given a simple diet. The bone mineral density was tested with the help of a densimeter before beginning yoga treatment. The test was repeated after 40 days of yoga.

Results

The effects of yoga and pranayama on various diseases are presented below as the combined outcome of the above studies.

Respiratory System and Related Diseases

Study 1: Sixty-one per cent of 970 patients at the six residential camps with irregular pulmonary function had significant improvement. Immediate improvement in forced vital capacity (FVC), maximum voluntary ventilation (MVV) and peak expiratory flow rate (PEFR) was seen.

Study 2: Forty-three per cent of 196 patients showed significant improvement in PFT level as per international standards.

Blood Circulation System (Cardio-Pulmonary System)

Study 1: Twenty-four per cent of 772 patients with irregular ECG before the camp showed positive improvement as per international standards.

The patients with abnormal ECG showed significant improvement in bradycardia, T-wave inversion, Atrial fibrillation, tachycardia, ectopia, ST (stress test) changes, heart block and inferior infarction levels. The electrocardiogram of LVH (left ventricular hypertrophy), anterior infarction, RVH, anteroseptal infarction, RBBB (right bundle branch block showing impaired transmission of electric impulses from the atrioventricular bundle to the right ventricle) and LBBB (left bundle branch block) did not show any improvement (Table 2).

The total cholesterol, HDL, LDL and triglyceride levels showed improvement among 82.9 per cent, 50 per cent, 86.5 per cent and 84.3 per cent patients, respectively (Table 3).

Study 3: Positive results were obtained in the tests conducted for cholesterol before and after the camp.

Anaemia

Study 2: Twenty-five per cent of 25 patients showed normal level, while the remaining showed significant improvement.

Blood Pressure

Study 1: About 65 per cent of 1,312 patients with high blood pressure witnessed a fall to normal value less than 120/80 mm Hg (Table 4). Average systolic blood pressure decreased from 158.54 to 150.12. Average diastolic blood pressure decreased from 92.29 to 87.21.

Study 2: Seventy-three per cent of the participants reported normal blood pressure after the camp.

Study 3: Positive results were obtained in the tests conducted for blood pressure before and after the camp.

Endocrine Glands (Internal Secretion Glands) and Related Diseases

Study 1: The patients with irregular triiodothyronine (T_3), thyroxin (T_4) and TSH levels showed 100 per cent improvement.

Study 2: Seventy-six per cent of 112 patients with hypothyroidism gained normal levels, and 55 per cent of 20 patients with hyperthyroidism before the camp acquired normal hormone level afterwards.

Diabetes

Study 1: Thirty-nine per cent of 2,240 patients with a high fasting glucose level before the camps showed improvement (Table 5). Positive changes were seen even in the common symptoms of diabetes like polyuria, polyphagia, polydipsia, weakness and painful discharge.

Study 2: About 46 per cent of 779 patients with a high blood sugar level showed considerable improvement (all the patients were asked to stop medication before the beginning of study).

Obesity

Study 1: A majority of the obese patients reduced their weight by 5–10 kg within one week.

Study 2: As many as 90 per cent of 362 obese patients lost weight up to 5 kg in one week.

Study 3: Forty-two per cent of 238 patients lost more than 2 kg. Maximum weight loss was 9.5 kg.

Kidney Diseases

Study 1: Eighty-eight per cent of 66 patients with an irregular level of serum creatinine showed improvement.

Study 2: In 51 per cent of the 1,080 patients, improvement was noticed in serum urea level, whereas creatinine level showed improvement in 61 per cent of the patients.

Liver Function

Study 2: As per international standards, total bilirubin, ALP (alkaline phosphatase – used to help detect liver disease where damaged liver cells release increased amounts of ALP into the blood), SGPT (Alanine aminotransferase) and SGOT (Aspartate aminotransferase) showed improvement in, respectively, 50 per cent, 67 per cent, 56 per cent and 64 per cent of patients.

Arthritis

Study 2: Forty-five per cent of 110 patients witnessed improvement in haemoglobin. The patients showed 45 per cent and 55 per cent improvement in RA factor and uric acid, respectively.

Study 3: The efficiency and confidence level in 18 male osteoporosis patients was, respectively, 4.2 per cent and 99.7 per cent. The figures in case of female patients for the same disease were 4.0 per cent and 99.7 per cent, respectively. Among the patients of osteopenia, males showed efficiency and confidence level of 4.7 per cent and 99.7 per cent, respectively, whereas females showed 3.7 per cent and 99.7 per cent, respectively. Thus, the T-score of bone mineral density showed considerable improvement along with increasing strength of bone after 40 days of yoga practice.

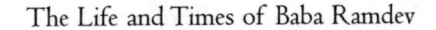

Cancer

Study 2: The analysis of results after the camp showed 50 per cent clinical improvement among 12 patients in AFP, PFA and CA-125.

Overall, these trials showed that through the process of pranayama we can increase the normal volume of ventilation by ten times without any physical exercise. When we increase physical activity, the body demands and uses more oxygen, whereas in pranayama the amount of oxygen increases without increasing the carbon dioxide level. This purifies blood and ensures that every cell in the body gets sufficient amount of oxygen. The oxygenation creates energy by producing adenosine tri-phosphate (ATP) for proper nourishment of the cells. This in turn retards the degeneration of cells caused by necrosis. Thus, pranayama can be considered as the best antioxidant to remove the secretions from the body so that respiratory diseases like tuberculosis, cough and asthma can be cured.

Thousands of people in queues awaiting their turn to meet Baba

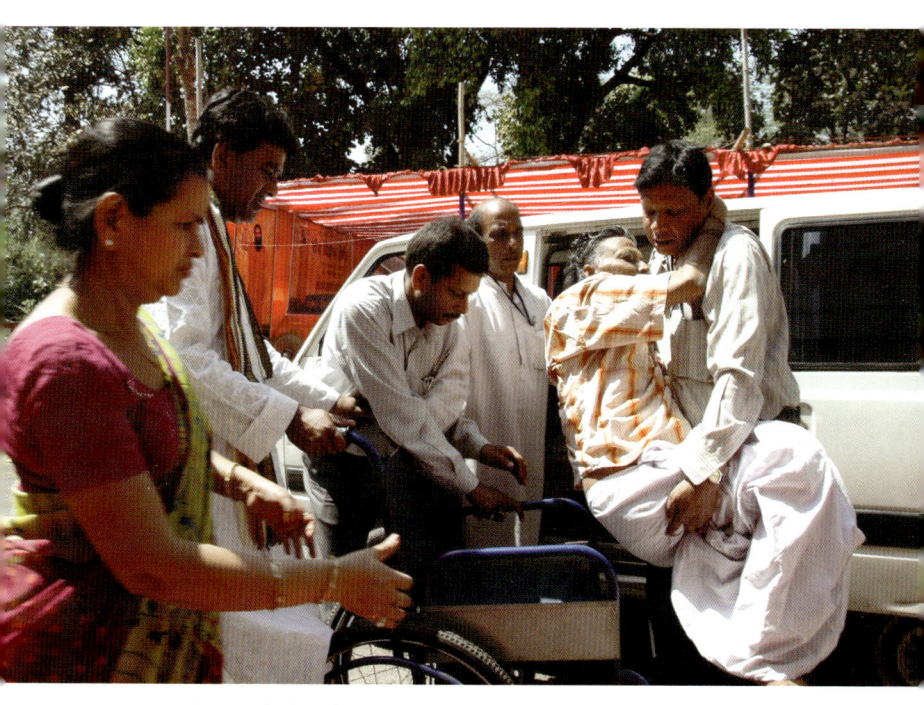

One of the devotees carrying his ailing father to get the blessings of Baba

Baba showering rose petals on his followers at one of his camps

Baba in a joyful mood at a gathering

Baba's ashram at Haridwar

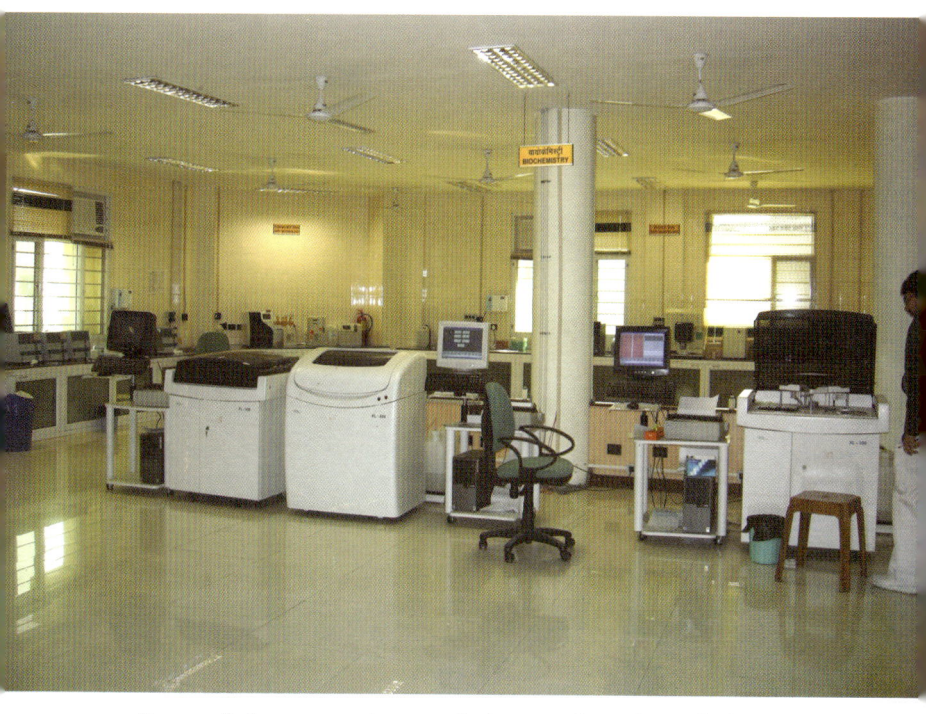

State-of-the-art equipment being used in the Baba's ashram hospital at Haridwar

Large number of foreign nationals attend Baba's yoga camps regularly

Baba greets them all with folded hands

Table 1: Results of pulmonary function test (PFT)

Residential Camp	No. of people with irregular PFT	No. of people with irregular PFT after camp	Number of patients benefited	Percentage of patients benefited
1	95	40	55	57.8
2	132	51	81	61.4
3	230	80	150	65.2
4	235	93	142	60.4
5	207	86	121	58.5
6	71	27	44	62.0
Total/Overall	970	377	593	61.0

Source: Tables 1 to 5 have been derived from Acharya Balakrishna, *Yoga in Synergy with Medical Science*, Divya Prakashan, Patanjali Yogpeeth, Haridwar, 2005.

Table 2: Ranking of indicators of cardio-pulmonary diseases according to percentage of patients benefited

Ailment/disease	No. of people before camp	No. of people after camp	Number of patients benefited	Percentage of patients benefited
Tachycardia	119	62	57	48.0
Ectopia	74	46	28	37.8
Atrial fibrillation	3	2	1	33.3
Bradycardia	55	39	16	29.0
T-wave inversion	167	132	35	21.0
Heart block	11	9	2	18.2
Inferior infarction	15	13	2	13.3
ST changes	71	64	7	9.9
RBBB	82	75	7	8.5
LVH	34	32	2	5.9
Anterior infarction	23	22	1	4.3
LBBB	33	32	1	3.0
LAD	29	29	0	0.0
Anteroseptal infarction	7	7	0	0.0
RVH	6	6	0	0

Table 3: Changes in total cholesterol, HDL, LDL and triglycerides

Parameter	No. of people with irregular level before	No. of people with irregular level after camp	Number of patients benefited	Percentage of patients benefited
Total cholesterol	789	135	654	82.9
HDL	66	33	33	50.0
LDL	156	21	135	86.5
Triglycerides	1,420	223	1,197	84.3

Table 4: Changes in blood pressure

Range (mm Hg)	No. of people before camp	No. of people after camp	Number of patients benefited	Percentage of patients benefited
> 180/110	25	7	18	72.0
160/100 to 180/110	78	41	37	47.4
130/90 to 160/100	637	173	464	72.8
120/80 to 130/90	572	241	331	57.9
Total/Overall	1,312	462	850	64.8

Table 5: Changes in fasting glucose

Parameter	People with irregular level before camp	People with irregular level after camp	Number of patients benefited	Percentage of patients benefited
Fasting glucose	2,240	1,362	878	39.2

Three Specialized Studies

Apart from the above-mentioned clinical trials, Divya Yogpeeth also conducted two specialized studies to assess the effect of yoga and pranayama on psychophysical aspects of stress hormones as well as on psychophysiological aspects of healthy people and those exhibiting metabolic diseases. A large-size survey was undertaken to get feedback from the practitioners of yoga and pranayama on the impact of these practices on psychosomatic profile, spiritual and social awakening, and changes in attitudes and lifestyle.

Study I: Psychophysical effects of stress hormones

For this, 119 healthy adults were selected who were not suffering any addiction. They were divided into two groups. Group A (study group, number 63) was taught pranayama and made to practise it for at least two hours everyday. Group B (control group, number 56) was restricted from practising pranayama. After the camp, the participants of Group A were asked to continue the practice of pranayama for one hour or two hours daily for a period of three months. The participants of Group B were asked to lead a normal life devoid of pranayama practice. The study was conducted by senior scientists of Swami Vivekananda Yoga Anusandhana Samsthana University, Bangalore (now Bengaluru); Sanjay Gandhi Post-Graduate Institute of Medical Sciences, Lucknow; and Sahara India Medical Institute, Lucknow.

On the basis of fixed parameters, blood samples were collected on the first day and the tenth day (end of camp), and again in the third month without practice of yoga. After nightlong fasting, heparin was used (sodium heparin 400–1000 Iu/ml) and blood samples were taken to test the presence of beta-endorphin in EDTA (ethylenediamine tetracetatic acid – used to bind metal ions in chelation therapy, e.g., for mercury, and the most reliable method for detecting excessive lead stored in body). Blood sugar from blood was collected to test the presence of fat, creatinine, nitrogen factors, SGPT, breast-simulating hormone, ACTH (Adrenocorticotropic hormone – a polypeptide tropic hormone secreted by the anterior pituitary gland and produced in response to biological stress) and cortisol.

Results

On the basis of baseline for control and test groups, there was no difference between blood cortisol, breast-simulating hormone, endorphin and ACTH level. After 10 days, the endorphin blood mean and breast-simulating hormone had reduced, but the value was insignificant. The participants of yoga group showed significant drop in weight, basal metabolism, systolic blood pressure and diastolic blood pressure. There was a significant change in the mean of breast simulator, endorphin and cortisol after three months. The stress hormone level had reduced in participants compared to the ten-day supervised short-term practice of pranayama. On the other hand, the control group practising pranayama at home without supervision did not show significant reduction in stress hormone levels. Therefore, there is a need to study supervised regular practice of pranayama on stress.

Study 2: Study of psychophysiological effects of yoga training on healthy volunteers and those with metabolic syndrome

This study, conducted at an eight-day yoga training camp, was intended to examine the effect of yoga and pranayama on the capacity of voluntary breath-holding, autonomic balance with a shift towards parasympathetic dominance, autonomic reactions to physical provocation like hand grip, motor functions (viz. strength of grip, speed for repetitive movement and fine motor skills), and performance in a task for focused and selective attention.

The study was focused on two groups of 100 participants each – healthy volunteers and those with metabolic syndrome (high level of body mass index, cholesterol and obesity). The yoga modules consisted of seven light exercises, seven basic asanas, seven pranayamas, yoga *nidra* and meditation. The participants were asked to do self-practice for the next three months after the camp.

The medical status of the participants was analysed using the following parameters: heart rate, galvanic skin resistance, digit pulse volume and respiration, and hand grip and tapping speeds, as well as psychological factors for testing the six-letter cancellation test (SLCT) and symptoms checklist. The motor skills were determined using the O'Connor Tweezer Dexterity Test, in which the participants were asked to lift metallic pins with small tweezers, with the hand they normally work with, and place them in small holes of metallic plates with maximum speed for four minutes. The number of pins successfully placed in the plate was taken as the dexterity score. Hand-grip dynamometer was used to test the gripping strength of both hands. The participants were asked to press an object with maximum strength several times. For measuring tapping speed (fast and repetitive movement of front and wrist part of hand), the participants were asked to tap on alternate circles on paper with pencil for 60 seconds. The total number of tappings made on both circles was counted.

Two types of tests were employed to study the psychological variables – symptoms checklist (SCL–90) to measure the physical symptoms caused by mental condition and those related to stress; and six-letter cancellation test (SLCT) to measure the concentration and scanning skills based on observation. In this test, six targets were to be cancelled. The alphabets were to be arranged randomly in 22 rows and 14 columns. The participants were asked to cancel six target letters within 90 seconds as many times as possible. The total number of cancelled letters and wrong cancellations were noted.

Results

Healthy Volunteers

I. Autonomic and respiratory variables

Skin resistance: There was a significant increase in galvanic skin resistance in the yoga group at the end of the yoga camp, but there was no change in the control group. This indicates a reduction in simulation of sweat glands. The sweat glands are considered to be simulators of the sympathetic cholinergic system.

Heart rate: At the end of the camp, there was a significant increase in heart rate in the control group, whereas there was no difference in the yoga group. The respiratory rate, however, was even in both the groups. This shows that factors responsible for anxiety are not associated with practice of yoga.

Blood pressure: The systolic blood pressure reduced by 3 mm Hg in the yoga group as well as in the control group. The diastolic blood pressure reduced by an average 3 mm Hg in the yoga group.

Autonomic factors: The changes in autonomic factors were assessed by posing a challenge to the participants. Isometric hand-grip strength that produces sympathetic rendition increased in both yoga and control groups on the last day of the camp in finger plethysmogram amplitude.

II. Motor tasks

Hand dexterity and speed tasks: Initial speed depends on the portion related to neck and spine. Dexterity and skill depend on the speed of movement of hands and shoulders, coordination of hands, and reflexes of eyes and fingers. This study shows that yoga improves the O'Connor Tweezer Dexterity performance. This weariness was less after the camp, compared to before the camp. Similarly, practice improved hand dexterity and reduced the weariness of small muscles of hands. Peg-board test used in speed tasks showed that excessive worry and weakness have an indirect relation to performance. Along with that, lower efficiency of speed-task tendency is correlated to mental worry. After six weeks of yoga practice, there was a considerable decrease in the symptoms of worry in the patients. Hence, the effect of yoga in reducing worry in the present study can be responsible for improving the score in dexterity test.

Hand-grip strength denotes muscular strength and patience. In case of hand-grip test, there was considerable improvement in the grip of left hand after the yoga camp. Not much change was observed in the right hand, which could be due to some fault in research planning. The improvement in hand-grip strength was due to practice of pranayama and reduction in oxygen requirement.

Thus, the study shows that healthy volunteers showed a lower level of anxiety after yoga practice, both during period of rest and when dealing with some problem. There was marked repeated improvement in speed tasks, fall in weariness, improved tolerance and hand-grip strength. Also, yoga practice helped in mitigating the effects of repeated use of hands and wrist. The physical symptoms of mental disorders reduced and so did the feeling of stress due to surroundings, general atmosphere, food, season and routine.

Patients with metabolic syndrome

In case of people with metabolic syndrome, there was improvement in letter cancellation tasks, which proves that after yoga practice there is improvement in eye-and-hand coordination, visual scanning and selected mental abilities. The tapping speed increased in case of repeated movements, which shows that weariness in hands, wrists and fingers got reduced.

Study 3: Psychosomatic effects of yoga

This study intended to examine the effects of yoga on people with diverse social, cultural and geographical backgrounds. As many as 84,663 participants from India, England, America,

Thailand, Japan, Australia, Canada, Pakistan, Nepal, Bangladesh, Sri Lanka and UAE participated in this survey.

Results

I. Awareness about yoga

The source of awareness about yoga for 66 per cent of the participants was television, whereas 8 per cent learnt about it in a residential camp, 13 per cent in a non-residential yoga camp and another 13 per cent came to know about yoga from other sources. While 81 per cent of the participants confirmed practising yoga regularly, the rest 19 per cent were not regular practitioners.

II. Benefits of yoga and pranayama in treatment of diseases

Obesity: Around 95 per cent people were able to shed weight and experienced total or partial relief from obesity-related diseases.

High blood pressure: Among 19 per cent of participants suffering from high blood pressure, 96 per cent confirmed the positive effect of yoga and pranayama in controlling blood pressure. Only 4 per cent said that blood pressure increased after yoga practice.

Arthritis: Among 23 per cent of the participants suffering from this problem, 93 per cent reported total or partial gain from yoga and pranayama.

Diabetes: Among 28 per cent of the diabetic participants in the sample, 95 per cent confirmed partial or total benefits.

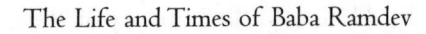

Heart disease: Among 14 per cent of the participants suffering from heart diseases, 94 per cent said yoga and pranayama brought about partial or total benefit.

Asthma: Among 12 per cent of the participants suffering from asthma, 96 per cent said they experienced partial or total benefit.

Kidney diseases: Among 19 per cent participants suffering from kidney problems, 94 per cent reported partial or total benefit.

Spondylitis: Among 16 per cent of the participants suffering from this problem, 95 per cent reported partial or total benefit.

Skin diseases: In the sample, 13 per cent of the participants were suffering from skin diseases, and 92 per cent of them found yoga and pranayama partially or totally beneficial.

Liver and stomach diseases: Among 31 per cent of the participants suffering from these diseases, 94 per cent confirmed that pranayama had brought about partial or total benefit.

III. Change in mental condition with yoga and pranayama

Mental stress: Yoga and pranayama reduced stress level in 48 per cent of the participants, whereas 42 per cent claimed not to have gained any benefit. In fact, 10 per cent said that stress increased even after practice.

Positive attitude: The practice of yoga and pranayama increased positive attitude among 62 per cent of the participants, whereas 5 per cent said the level of positive attitude reduced. On the other hand, 33 per cent of the participants felt no impact.

Memory: Yoga and pranayama improved memory and concentration in 47 per cent of the participants, while 49 per cent felt no impact. For 4 per cent of the respondents, the impact was negative.

IV. Change in family life

Mutual love: Among the participants, 60 per cent agreed that yoga has changed the quality of their family life and there is now a greater intensity of love and warmth in the family.

Happiness: In the sample, 68 per cent said that yoga and pranayama have increased their feeling of happiness, whereas 32 per cent said that their practice has helped them in attaining self-realization, freeing them from unknown fears and death.

Respect towards elders: Sixty-two per cent of the participants agreed that yoga and pranayama have helped them in their attitude towards elders.

V. Change in social life

Interest in social work: Yoga has inspired 60 per cent of the participants to take up some kind of social work.

Charity for the poor and destitute: Of the total participants, 67 per cent showed inclination towards taking up charity and public-welfare activities, and reaching out to the downtrodden.

VI. Changes in lifestyle

Vegetarianism: Among 27 per cent of the participants who were non-vegetarians, 73 per cent quit non-vegetarian food.

Alcohol addiction: A high 85 per cent of the participants quit alcohol after practising yoga and pranayama.

Fast food: Of the total participants who practised yoga and pranayama, 69 per cent quit consuming fast food like pizzas, burgers and potato chips, and 25 per cent were able to reduce consumption of the same. Also, 63 per cent of the participants were able to get rid of their craving for cold drinks.

Multinational products: In the sample, 68 per cent of the newly enlightened participants stopped purchasing products of multinational corporations (MNCs).

VII. Spiritual awakening

As many as 97 per cent of the participants agreed that practising yoga and pranayama helped to improve their spirituality level.

VIII. About Divya Yogpeeth

Eighty-three per cent of the participants were of the view that the institute was playing an excellent role in promoting yoga and good health, while another 14 per cent said that the work done was very good. Only 3 per cent said that the work of the institution was unsatisfactory.

Scepticism of the Rejectionist Medical Fraternity

The seer's relationship with the mainstream medical fraternity is characterized by extreme antagonism on the part of the latter. The Indian Medical Association (IMA) has become highly critical of his views against allopathic medicine and his claim of treating serious diseases like cancer through yoga and pranayama. To mobilize doctors across India, the association wrote an open letter to them in 2006 accusing the seer of misguiding people. According to an IMA official, 'There was no dispute over the benefits of yoga for health, but Ramdev is presenting yoga like pop music. It is wrong because it is not scientifically proved yet. His medicines have not been scientifically tested before their launch in the market.'[3]

The then health minister, Dr Anbumani Ramadoss, also joined the fray by denouncing the claims of the seer. According to him, it is time to put an end to such claims, and to deter home-grown healers who say they can treat diseases like AIDS. He also proposed amending the Drugs and Magical Remedies Act to make it illegal to advertise claims for invalidated cures, either allopathic or alternative. In view of this, in December 2006, the health ministry sent a notice to at least 80 organizations, including Ramdev's to desist from making 'false' claims on cures. According to Ramdev, yoga and Ayurveda together can only alleviate the suffering from AIDS – not cure it completely. As claimed by him, the patients who followed his regimen were later tested at the All India Institute of Medical Sciences, New Delhi, as also at the Johns Hopkins Hospital, USA. Their CD4 (cluster of differentiation-4) count was found to be less than others. Also, at a residential camp held in Yoga Gram, Haridwar, in June 2008, several cancer patients recounted first-hand stories of their successful management of blood cancer, prostrate cancer, breast cancer, pituitary gland, brain tumours and leukaemia through the practice of pranayama.

The controversy thrown up by Ramadoss soon turned into a strong criticism of the country's health system, as seen in the comments made by several concerned individuals. According to them, the health minister should first focus on the condition of the government hospitals and the private hospitals, rather than criticize yoga. Thousands of these hospitals are starved of doctors and good medicines, and are infamous for their bad hygiene and inhuman environment. As evidence, a TV channel even showed how the patients were given adulterated food and milk. Even the staff was caught stealing half the gas out of cylinders and selling the same in the market. In another TV report, it was shown that the management of a private hospital threw a patient's body in a ditch as they were unable to save the patient and were desperate to avoid a police enquiry at all cost.

Further, the minister may have forgotten that various governments have been responsible for encouraging some of the ills that Baba Ramdev is talking about. He can contribute more by banning wine shops, junk-food restaurants, pizza joints, cigarette companies, and sugar mills generating molasses. In a strange turnaround, however, Ramadoss subsequently established links with Ramdev and discussed ways to popularize alternative health care and spread awareness of yoga in the rural areas, and decided on a concerted effort to combat the spread of alcohol, tobacco and junk food in the country.[4]

Despite the controversy, Ramdev exhibits honesty towards the efficacy of his yoga and states that he is merely a *sadaka* (practitioner). While he vouches for the effectiveness of his key pranayamas, he is yet to establish the efficacy of the supplementary pranayamas promoted by him. For instance, in the case of Nadi Shodhan Pranayama, he asks his followers to practise it with caution as he has not got sufficient evidence for its stated efficacy in the scriptures. Only after a prolonged study on individuals and identifying its most appropriate technique, its duration and end-results, can it be safely recommended for practise by all. Thus, Ramdev's work does not represent a definite end to yogic exploration. Incidentally, the seer is also honest about his fears of the unknown. When he faced a murderous attempt some years ago, he came close to death. 'For a few moments, I felt scared like any other living being on the edge of dying,' he later said at a gathering.

Notes and References

1. Ramdev – interview, *Yog Sandesh*, (January) Divya Mandir Trust, Haridwar, 2006.

2. Acharya Balkrishana, *Yoga in Synergy with Medical Science*, Divya Prakashan, Patanjali Yogpeeth, Haridwar, 2007.

3. 'Ramdev Is a Quack: IMA', www.indiastandard.com/News/Social/Health/Ramdev-is-a-quack-says-IMA-chief.html.

4. 'Ramadoss Meets Ramdev to Promote "Alternative Healthcare"', www.expressindia.com/latest-news/Ramadoss-meets-Ramdev-to-promote-alternative-healthcare/324485/.

Chapter 5

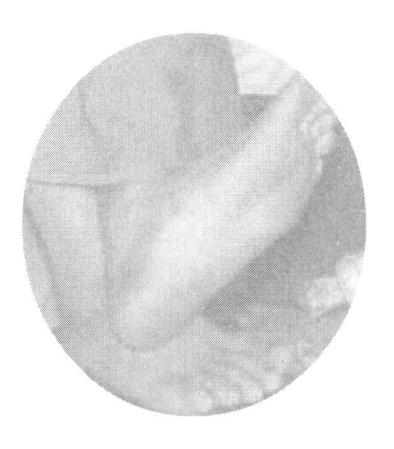

Ramdev's Mass-Awakening Doctrine

योग व्यक्ति को स्वावलम्बी
एवं आत्मनिर्भर बनाता है

… while our country is an emerging power in science and technology, age-old frivolous superstitions and practices like astrology continue to perpetuate the decline of the society and tend to eclipse the purity of Indian spiritual thought. 'Why do the planets like Rahu, Ketu and Sani influence the Indians? Why don't they affect Japan, Germany, Pakistan, America, etc.? …'

Having gained the attention of a wide section of people as the ultimate health messiah, Ramdev has set for himself a purpose higher than that of a healer of the sick. He has transformed his yoga doctrine into concerted activism in order to reinstate in the popular mind an ideology of national reconstruction for building a healthy, spiritually raised, self-reliant India.[1] In a very significant way, his doctrine carries encoded messages of national resurgence – attempting to merge the synergies of spiritual awakening into the concerns of social and national rejuvenation. In fact, extending the yoga way of life from 'universal health' goal to several other critical issues affecting the modern society is a unique feature of Ramdev's philosophy. For him, the yoga way of life demands responsibility towards both oneself and the society at large.

This ideological thrust is aimed at systematically breaking down the current inward-looking Indian cultural and religious identities and the self-gratifying mindset, and thus preparing the people at large for unleashing a powerful movement for mass awakening. He has built its narrative around the notion of spiritual enlightenment, taking up a well-informed discourse on the human re-connection with the Self and the outside world. Indeed, the strong spiritual and cultural bearing of this common-looking man is creating a strong affinity in the collective consciousness. The seer's intense critique of the age-old orthodoxy and the social tensions and suffering being caused by it has now found acceptance among a large section of people.

Ramdev's doctrine, spread over innumerable discourses and essays, is an ideological rendering on an ambitious national awakening and rejuvenation project, conceived by the seer in response to the ills and inadequacies of a largely failed nation-state. The basic edifice around which he builds his radical proposition is the concept of 'spiritually-awakened-and-manifested socialism'. This political philosophy envisages imbuing mass spiritual awakening with the emancipatory goals of socialism, the wider ecological concerns and the anti-globalization movements. In the Indian context, the concept of spiritual socialism envisages a combination of Vedanta philosophy and the Gandhian norms of swadeshi, simplicity and austerity. Its aims are to ensure social equality through respect and service to fellow human beings and promote ecologically sustainable development. Since an all-pervading God is in all beings in spiritual socialism, no one is superior to others.[2]

We shall now discuss this doctrine in detail.

Ramdev's mass-awakening doctrine is built around a grand vision of a civilizational project, which envisages setting forth sequential manifestation of a set of transformations in people in the way they perceive and change themselves and the world around them. The anticipated transformations are:

1. Reaching the perpetual spiritual state
2. Cultivating rational mindset with spiritual insights
3. Rising above organized religion to dharma
4. Liberation from neo-colonialism

5. Nurturing inter-community tolerance
6. Countering media-triggered cultural subjugation
7. Choosing the indigenous science-swadeshi-ecology integral
8. Articulating environmental, agricultural and animal welfare concerns
9. Empowering women
10. Reforming education
11. Rising above casteism and reversing reservation policies
12. Containing economic disparities and growing social disquiet
13. Fighting corruption – the ill of all ills
14. Sacralizing the nation – towards a spiritual nationalistic resurgence.

Reaching the Perpetual Spiritual State

The ideal yogic state as perceived by the past spiritual masters is the state in which an individual acquires a physically endurable and spiritually awakened persona – the foremost precondition in understanding the way he perceives his well-being and his place in the world, and identifies the ideological distortions that have been leading to his unhappiness and suffering. Sri Aurobindo laid out the psychological insights and practices to achieve this state. The Poorna Yoga evolved by him sought to promote an inner self-development by which each one discovers the One Self in all and reach a consciousness higher than the mental – a spiritual and supramental consciousness that will transform and divinize human nature. According to Swami Vivekananda, the science of yoga can help each one to grow and strengthen his personality. The utility of this science is to bring out the perfect man. This science wants each one to be strong, to take the work into one's own hands instead of leaving it in the hands of nature, and get beyond this little life.[3] Swami Dayananda, too, laid out the means to attain salvation or freedom in terms of practice of yoga, acquisition of knowledge, true knowledge, purity of thought and deeds, and the like.[4]

Ramdev also postulates the ideal spiritual state as the manifestation of one's true self-realization or virtually a rebirthing through the noble truth of yoga. According to the seer, with the power of yoga, unhappiness and other negative thoughts are removed and the soul gets the ultimate happiness and a peaceful abode.

Cultivating Rational Mindset with Spiritual Insights

Scientific rationality as demanded by modern science's preoccupations with laboratory-driven objectivity reflects its demand to erase the past wisdoms and ensure a future on its own terms. But the other rationality, *viveka*, as propounded in the Advaitin traditions is part of one's self-realization towards knowing the causes of ignorance, wrong views and human suffering in the man–nature relationship. Swami Vivekananda in his famous lecture on Practical Vedanta delivered in London in 1896 had said: 'All great developments come from thinking, from discrimination – *viveka*. We need to educate our children with the capacity to think for themselves; we have to instill into them the scientific temper and the humanistic temper. What we want is progress, development, realization. No theories ever made men higher. No amount of books can help us to become purer. The only power is in realization, and that lies in ourselves and comes from thinking. *Let men think.*'[5]

In his concept of 'science and Sanskrit', Vivekananda advocated a synthesis of the best aspects of the traditional Hindu and western systems of education, based on an equal, reciprocal exchange of eastern spirituality and western materialism. The swami did not approve of practices like parapsychology and astrology, saying that this form of curiosity does not help in spiritual progress but actually hinders it.[6] Swami Dayananda also discouraged dogma and symbolism, and encouraged scepticism in beliefs that run contrary to common sense and logic. According to the sage, the Truth is a quality of being in agreement with the reality and all that is opposite should not be considered as Truth. Astrology, as far as arithmetic, geometry, etc. is concerned, is science. Misfortune or fortune have nothing to do with the planets; the sufferings or the good fortunes are due to the past and present karmas. Astrology used for predicting is a failure, and to indulge in any method to avoid misfortunes is rubbish. He also pronounced superstitions as self-serving.[7]

Ramdev's views on rationality echo the concerns of these thinkers – only thorough questioning, enquiry and deep meditation lead to spiritual or complete growth of man, from *vyaktitva* to *vikasita vyaktitva*. He asks for a careful examination of whatever is observed and learnt. According to him, 'The people carry loads of many weakening superstitions, obscurantist ideas, and many anti-human practices, to shed. The sages of the Upanisads were moved by a passion for truth and a passion for human happiness and welfare. They achieved their purposes through rational questioning and inquiry and deep meditation. We can appreciate the greatness of our own culture, our own spirituality only when we develop a critical, truth-seeking, scientific mind. The Vedanta emphasizes the truth of our essential oneness and a rational, questioning attitude. Therefore, our education must help our children to develop such a critical, scientific, truth-seeking attitude. What is truth? What is a true life? How to live a true life and not a false life? This kind of questing and questioning attitude will help to bring out the highest possibilities hidden in our children; and through such transformed children, our whole nation will develop its true wealth, namely, human energy resources.'

The master further says that a scientific temper should be combined with a humanistic temper. Both these together constitute the spiritual growth of man. They constitute the critical search for truth and the passion to ensure human happiness and welfare. Therefore, love and concern for others become a by-product of this spiritual growth from individuality to personality.

According to the seer, there is an utmost need to transform – through education – the nation into a thoughtful, critical, scientific community imbued with the passion for truth and for total human welfare. Our children will imbibe the capacity to appreciate their nation's great wealth of spiritual and cultural heritage, and to brighten the *lives* of our people at large. This is what will integrate man with man, irrespective of caste, creed, race or sex, and make our nation truly great.

The seer is highly critical about succumbing to beliefs that are not based on true knowledge. According to him, while our country is an emerging power in science and technology, age-old frivolous superstitions and practices like astrology continue to perpetuate the decline of the society and tend to eclipse the purity of Indian spiritual thought. 'Why do the planets like Rahu, Ketu and Sani influence the Indians? Why don't they affect Japan, Germany, Pakistan, America, etc.? If there were spirits and ghosts, then we would not have required soldiers on the borders. This is only an imagination,' argues the saffron-clad rationalist.

Rising above Organized Religion to Dharma

According to Swami Vivekananda, priestcraft is the bane of India as it is by nature cruel and heartless. Where priestcraft arises, religion goes down. We must give up the idea of privilege, and only then will religion come. Swami Dayananda was also one of the first reformers to bring to the fore the distortions caused in Hinduism since ages under the priests' self-aggrandizement. According to him, Brahmins subverted the whole system of classes and orders, and based it on the mere accident of birth, instead of on merit, character and works of the people. Dayananda, while unequivocally condemning all kinds of rituals, pronounced the concept of dharma: while religion is a specific system of belief and worship, dharma means duty. In 'Beliefs and Disbeliefs' (concluding chapter of his work *Satyarath Prakash*), he said, 'I accept as Dharma whatever is in full conformity with impartial justice, truthfulness and the like; he, who after careful thinking, is ever ready to accept truth and reject falsehood, who counts the happiness of others as he does that of his own self, him I call just.'[8]

Like his spiritual mentors, Ramdev too has challenged the prevailing decadence that is polluting ancient Hindu thought and practices. According to him, 'Today, whatever we are getting in the name of Vedas and Vedic culture, is leading to criminal mentality. The politicians, pujaris, priests are collectively responsible. They all are creating differences between people and dividing the society. God cannot be obtained by sitting in the temples, mosques and churches made after bloodshed. God is pleased with love, not sacrifice. Belief and faith in existence is belief in existence of god or theism. See the unseen in the seen, the large in the small, and the tree in the seed. The dwarf is also the giant.' Further, the seer does not believe that God resides in the temple; he resides within us and the body is the real place of worship, and therefore, it is our responsibility to keep it healthy and blissful. His paramount concern is restoration of the Self and its relationship with the world.

Some of the seer's followers often complain to him that they have worshipped God for the whole of their lives but that the Almighty has not given them darshan. The swami's answer is very apt and forthcoming: 'God is unperceivable because if He reveals Him in front of man, this lowly creature will say – Oh, it is like that! It was not worth the effort!! It is in the nature of man to underestimate what he gets. God's aura and power is in its invisibility, and it resides in us only. Reaching a blissful and love-filled state is the only way to realise Him.'

Liberation from Neo-Colonialism

As an essential thrust of his doctrine, Ramdev has raised a powerful ideological critique of the banes of westernization and their corrupting influence on Indian minds. According to him, the tyranny of the sensate and the compulsive self-gratification triggered by nineteenth-century scientific materialism is creating harmful effects on Indian culture and lifestyle. He wants Indians (and other people of the world as well) to get over the western fast-food culture, and like a true Gandhian, he vehemently condemns non-vegetarian food, alcohol and drug addiction. According to him, 'Killing innocent, dumb creatures is as big a crime as killing a human being. An animal can neither go to a police station to register a complaint nor to a court to fight the case. When you kill a living being,

Ramdev's Mass-Awakening Doctrine

feelings like hatred, revenge, fear and pain arise within it, and good feelings like affection, sympathy [and] love [are] lost.'

Following in the footsteps of Mahatma Gandhi, who had dreamt of complete alcohol prohibition in the country, Ramdev considers this vice as one of the biggest enemies of the society, destroying man's wealth and life. The government's approach on liquor prohibition lacks conviction. Popularization of yoga is the only solution for propelling individuals and society towards healthy living, says the seer.[9] The youth is also getting trapped in the whirlpool of drug addiction. People practising yoga do not fall into the trap of drug addiction and lust.

The seer has also extended his 'western lifestyle' critique to the wider issue of self-reliance, and has argued for reverting to India's economic policies through the 1950s, '60s and '70s – a major concern of the country's Left parties in those years. Citing vast historical evidence, he points out that beginning with the first agent of the East India Company in 1615, Thomas Roe, to the first governor-general, Warren Hastings, to the last governor-general, Mountbatten, a foreign company robbed property and wealth worth 278 lakh crores of rupees for 350 years. Now, more than 5,000 foreign companies are operating in our country, ravaging big chunks of Indian wealth every year. They produce flour, salt, water, cold drinks, juice, chips, soaps, oils, creams, shoes, sandals and garments, all with zero technology (these are the goods in which no special technique or science is used), and sell them at inflated prices, thus taking away crores of rupees from the country.

Thus, the seer's doctrine reflects, in a way, the growing clash between the consumerist lifestyle of the westernized ruling class and associated wealth appropriation on the one hand, and the desperations of the masses left far behind by the so-called virtues of current liberalization policies, on the other. According to him, the multinational companies are playing havoc with the country's economy base, making it dependent on alien foreign technology and capital. He asks his fellowmen to fight tooth and nail this kind of economic enslavement perpetuated by the curse of globalization. He implores his fellow citizens to take the vow that they will no longer use the daily-use products made by foreign companies. Calling Leher Pepsi as 'Zeher Pepsi' (poison), he asks his followers to treat soft drinks as not more than toilet cleaners and advocates the boycott of wares dished out by MNCs – adopting Indian-made products instead. He is also perturbed by the vulgarity in cinema and on television – another evil adopted from western culture – and called Bollywood actresses characterless on his show: 'Bollywood actresses are characterless. They change partners with every film they do.' In contrast, he says, we do not find any kind of vulgarity in traditional dance.[10]

One of the hallmarks of Ramdev's 'self-reliance' call is his critique of the utter commercialization of modern medical system and its dependence on pharmaceutical MNCs. He wants to reinstate the philanthropic aspects of health system and its accessibility to the poor in the form of low-cost, patient-friendly solutions. 'The country should stop spending Rs. 15 trillion on allopathic medicines and switch to Ayurveda and yoga to ensure a clean environment,' he asserts.

Nurturing Inter-Community Tolerance

According to Ramdev, the basic reason for the prevalence of fundamentalist and casteist ideologies in the country is a lack of realization of the noble truth of universal oneness and compassion. A person trapped in the mindset of community, sect or religion manifests himself as an egoist stuck with prejudice and self-righteousness. Since yoga is not a community, sect or religion, a person who practises it gets free from any communal or sectarian or religious affinities, remains free from prejudices, and moves closer to the truth. He says, 'A person of good character does not fight in the name of religion, community, caste, language, etc. Therefore, I believe that yoga makes a person spiritual and chaste. Yoga brings a person closer to spirituality and spirituality builds his character.'

He further says, 'The great personalities do not have any religion or caste. They are born for the welfare of the entire mankind. Lord Mahavir and Gautam Buddha were not born only for the Jains or the Buddhists, respectively. Their character and personality was the ideal for the whole world. "*Mata bhoomi putroaham prithivya*" – this means this land is our mother and we are her sons. People feel proud to be a Hindu, a Muslim or a Sikh; it would be so nice if they feel proud to be Indians. Though people should be proud of their religion, they should also respect others' mothers.'

Countering Media-Triggered Cultural Subjugation

Like other spiritual thinkers, Ramdev is concerned about the fall of indigenous cultures being perpetuated by the globally dominant western cultural ideology and the powerful media and advertising entities. As a result, the content as well as form of today's media expressions in the country are flooded with misplaced sensuality, vulgarity and an overall artistic deterioration, be it the narrative, the music, the dance or the acting. These concerns of Ramdev, in fact, reflect a revival in the present times of the massive ideological debate on cultural subjugation by the Western media spearheaded by thinkers such as Herbert Schiller in the sixties.[11]

Choosing the Indigenous Science-Swadeshi-Ecology Integral

Ramdev's passionate discourses evoke a deep agony about the lost glory and pride of the people who have been colonized by the alien processes of modernization. Built into his doctrine is the need for a forceful cultural revival built around the iconography borrowed from ancient wisdom, as a counterpoint to the rapid onslaught of western culture and the manifestations of ill-conceived ideas of modernity.

Ramdev states and upholds the spiritual and cultural superiority of the colonized over the colonizing culture. His forceful call for spiritual and cultural revival is part of the ongoing processes of rediscovering the past wisdom and the vast repertoire of indigenous knowledge. In fact, the growing awareness about the cultural and medicinal basis of the health traditions and their built-in feature of being eco-friendly have compelled the vast majority to appreciate and respect the value of past knowledge systems.

Ramdev's emphasis on traditional scientific knowledge is catalysed by the very nature of this knowledge. This body of knowledge which a society acquires is based on the accumulation of experiences, informal experiments and intimate understanding of the environment in a given culture. It is owned by the local people who have nurtured and refined systems of knowledge of their own, relating to such diverse domains as geology, ecology, agriculture and health. It has helped in solving problems and contributed to the development of people's way of life in accordance with the changing time and environment. Such knowledge systems represent human creativity and man's inherent zeal for betterment of life through the production of objects of desire, both for economic use and recreation.

Baba performing light exercise

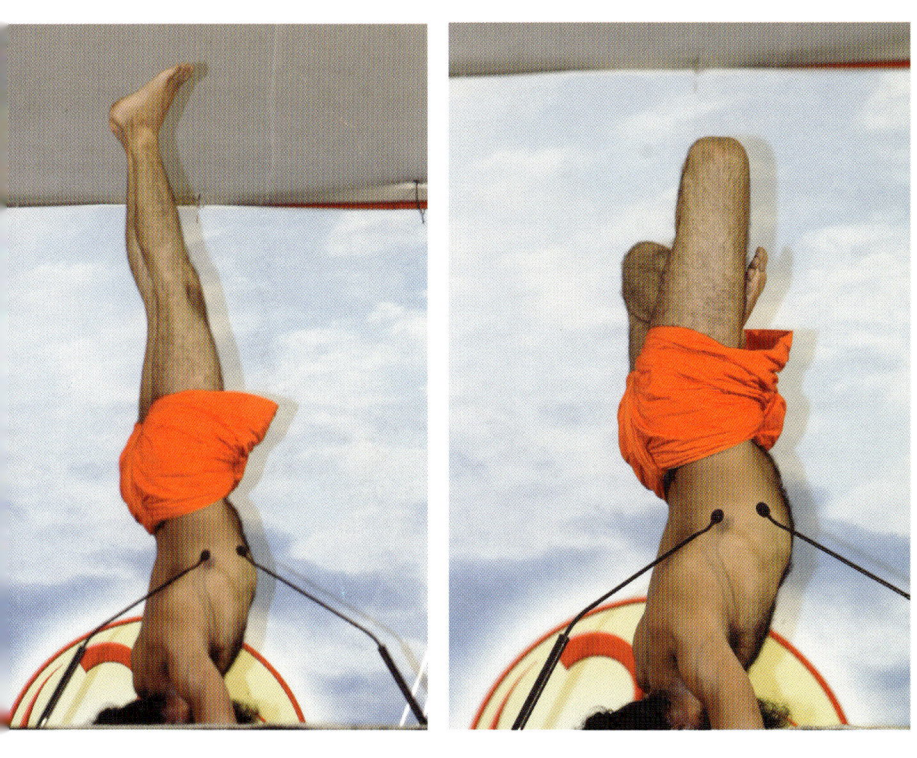

Baba performing Sirsasana (the head stand)

Baba performing Tolangulasana (the 'weighing scale' pose)

Baba performing Baddha Padmasana (the 'bound lotus' pose)

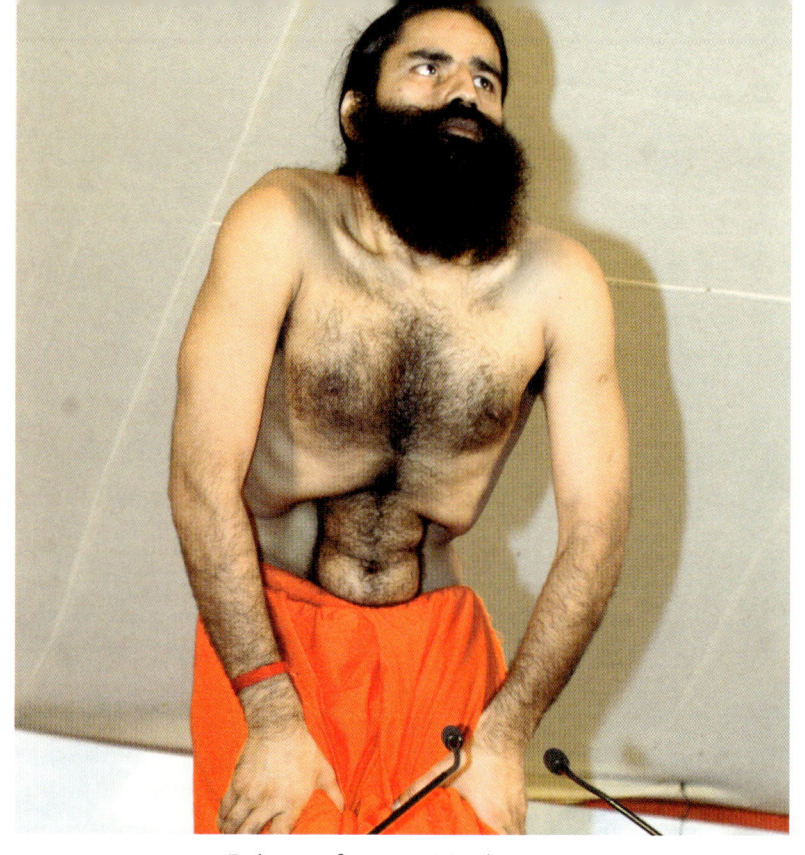

Baba performing Nauli Kriya

Baba performing Chakrasana (the 'upward bow' or 'wheel' pose)

Baba performing Kukkutasana (the 'cockerel' or 'rooster' pose)

Baba performing Mayurasana (the 'peacock' pose)

Indigenous knowledge derived from many years of experience have often been communicated through oral traditions and learned through family members and generations. It has its own well-established cognition and learning processes in which knowledge and associated skills are imparted through well-established ideas and practices to aspiring practitioners. In our ancient culture, technology represented the closeness of the relationship between arts, sciences and other forms of knowledge. The word 'technology' has been derived from two Greek words – *technique* (art) and *logos* (science). In Sanskrit, the word which comes close to 'technique' is *kala*. *Kala* means any practical art. In old Indian traditions, *kala* included not only dance, drama and painting, but also metallurgy, manufacturing and even development of dictionaries and encyclopedias.

Traditional knowledge can be categorized into many fields of knowledge such as agriculture, manufacturing, handicrafts, traditional medicine, natural resources and environment management, traditional art, community organizational management, language and literature, religion and traditions. It is time-tested, often over hundreds of years, and its worth is empirically tested and proven ('it happens this way').

Modern scientific knowledge, as we know, is the systematic body of man's knowledge established during the last 200 years or so, through the rigorous method of science – development of proven and verifiable scientific theories. While modern science laid out entirely new paths in the fields of astronomy, atomic physics, transport, and electronics and computers, traditional scientific knowledge has also been the basis of many science and technology areas like metallurgy, textiles, ceramics and dyes. Parts of the traditional knowledge system are often in areas that may not fall directly under the existing areas of modern science.

The keepers of modern knowledge have largely remained indifferent to the inherent value of the traditional knowledge system, on the argument that they do not have full-fledged theories backing it and so it cannot be judged or evaluated within the framework of modern science. However, of late, scientists the world over have recognized the importance of traditional knowledge and begun to realize that the tools and systems of modern science should be used to understand and validate the contents, practices and usefulness of traditional knowledge systems, be it in the areas of agriculture, health and medicine, or rural economic activities.

Today, Ramdev has emerged as the vanguard of indigenous knowledge or swadeshi, which was the key constituent of Mahatma Gandhi's vision for post-independent India. As an alternative to the current market-driven and globalized economic policies, the seer believes that ecologically reliable and indigenous science and technology should be the driving force for the country's progress. In this way, he finds his place among the galaxy of past path-breakers who spent their lifetimes in promoting an eco-conscious society based on traditional knowledge and wisdom.[12] Apart from the towering Gandhi himself, Vinoba Bhave, founder of the Sarvodaya Movement, Joseph Cornelius Kumarappa and several others also trod this path of alternative mode of social development.

Kumarappa (1892–1960) expounded his economic thoughts in the most holistic and original manner through his writings and work. He gave a call to shun using non-renewable resources of the earth which, he proclaimed, belonged to what can be termed as a 'bucket economy' (where the water is depleted as it is used up), and stressed that what we need is a 'river economy' (where water is being constantly replenished).

Baba Amte, another swadeshi icon, worked all his life towards creating a greater consciousness among tribal communities about what they can do to protect themselves against the onslaught of modernity, and campaigned for larger ecological issues. Sunderlal Bahuguna of 'Chipko Movement' fame pleaded for an alternative development strategy, whereby man and nature can exist in harmony. His Movement still symbolized a fight against ecological ruin and the destruction of life-support systems that indiscriminate industrialization has brought in its wake. Anna Hazare, the army man-turned-social worker, became a highly revered mass leader with the success of his model of a self-sufficient, collectively managed rural economy at Ralegan Siddhi village in Maharashtra, and his relentless crusade against corruption, untouchability and alcoholism.

C. V. Sashadari, an IIT (Indian Institutes of Technology) professor-turned-renegade, traced the roots of the environmental crisis to the fallacy of the Biblical notion of man's domination over nature. He realized that it made no sense to talk of ecology unless this foundational idea of western science was challenged. He grew up listening to his father reciting entire passages from the Vedas as well as French and English poetry with equal ease. He set up the Shri AMM Murugappa Chettiar Research Centre to study and evolve a viable ecosystem that would assure a meaningful quality of life for all living beings. He drew enormous inspiration from the experimental ways of Mahatma Gandhi and Kumarappa, whom he considered to be the archetypal Indian inventors.

Devendra Kumar, a product of the Gandhi–Sarvodaya tradition, was a direct disciple of J. C. Kumarappa and led the setting up of the Centre of Science for Villages at Wardha in Maharashtra, in 1976. The centre ushered in a new life to Maganwadi, where, four decades earlier, Gandhi and his colleagues had based the most intense phase of their endeavours for village industries. One of Kumar's key concerns was to counter the false impression that Gandhi was anti-science. N. D. Pandharipande, affectionately called Nadep Kaka, the inventor of Nadep bio-compost and other eco-compatible technologies, had a long association with Kumarappa and Mahatma Gandhi himself.

Ramdev represents a remarkable continuity to the works of these past luminaries, arguing for a return to swadeshi with renewed vigour in the current materialistic milieu. Like his earlier peers, he hails the ideology of ecologically sustainable and pro-people development because misguided policies have brought along several serious problems such as trade imbalance, urbanization, and cultural and environmental destruction, all of which affect the quality of life. According to the seer, the primary cause of these problems is a complete neglect of our indigenous knowledge, the splendid treasure that has played an important role in building the nation's unity and dignity. Now, it is time we turned back to our own philosophy, our own culture, and our own traditional knowledge.

Together, these traditions present a true sense of cultural togetherness in the modern-day world. Indeed, they can bring people closer to the inherent beauty and simplicity of their traditional local cultures. Therefore, we need an in-depth analysis of the parallelism of insights between the indigenous knowledge systems, on the one hand, and certain areas of modern science concerned with fundamental aspects, on the other. Our education system also needs to focus on this important issue, which it has neglected so far, Ramdev reminds. Several other contemporary thinkers and civil society activists also argue that the current economic and social development has placed undue emphasis on industrialization and technology.

Thus, in Ramdev's doctrine, spiritual self-realization itself manifests into ecological consciousness, which leads one to rise above materiality and respect nature. Therefore, his integrated eco-blueprint exhibits virtually all the key elements of the eco-global agenda: promoting a reduced consumption-based lifestyle, organic farming among farmers, afforestation, conservation of biodiversity, water and other resources, herbal food and medicine, and discovery of rare medicinal plant heritage. According to the seer, nearly 50 per cent of the diseases in India are being caused by alarming pollution of land, food, water, rivers, air and sky. Because of pollution in food, thought, mind and behaviour, the ills of disease, fear, corruption, crime and anarchy are spreading through the entire country. He says, 'The universe is purified by sacrificial fires, air is purified through planting of trees, the body is purified by water, mind is purified by truth, wealth is purified by donation, wisdom is purified by knowledge, and the soul is purified by study and penance. Even sage Patanjali had pronounced cleanliness to be the first rule for a yogi.'

Articulating Environmental, Agricultural and Animal Welfare Concerns

Ramdev has emerged as the new eco-guru in today's critical times of acute environment destruction and climate change. As the vanguard of pro-people eco-friendly development, he has expressed his concerns on the growing levels of air, water (particularly in the Indian rivers) and soil pollution, and its effects on health. The sage has also articulated a very strong critique of inorganic agriculture, substantiating it with massive official data as well as field reports carried out by his teams. According to him, technology-driven agricultural policies have not only marginalized millions of small Indian farmers but also have led to serious soil infertility. As a consequence, over the years, the yield per acre is decreasing rapidly forcing agricultural community to migrate to cities in search of livelihood. Further, 65 per cent of the cattle stock fed on polluted fodder in the country has been rendered infertile, resulting in drastic reduction in milk yield. The farmers sell their infertile cattle to the slaughter houses as indicated by the massive growth of meat industry and meat exports in recent years.

The sage has worked out an alternative sustainable development strategy for agriculture aimed at installing poison-free agriculture in the country. He has launched a nationwide campaign at the grassroots to de-pollute soil, promote organic farming and install a humanistic man–animal relationship. The key elements of the campaign are: conscientizing the farmers about the ills of chemical-based agriculture; establishing high productivity of organic farming through field cultivation/demonstration; and popularizing among farmers a field-tested compost technology for de-pollution of soil by which a bio-fertilizer can be produced in huge quantities using a mixture of herbs, cow dung, urine, sugar cake and soil dug beneath an old tree.

The seer has also vehemently opposed the introduction of Bt brinjal in the country arguing that by encouraging GM foods we are killing our traditional varieties and letting foreign seed companies take over the country's agriculture. Also, consumption of genetically modified food will lead to disorders of liver and kidney, he says.[13]

Empowering Women

Ramdev's views on women and strong advocacy of their active role in society reflect his respect for the fair sex. He urges women to set high goals for themselves and achieve everything they can. He inspires everyone to take an active role in serving the society. He asks every woman to awaken in herself the spirit of Sita, Jijabai and Rani Jhansi. As he says, 'If women demonstrate glare like fire, speed like air, patience like earth, coolness like water and broadness like space, they will be respected by all. This stands good for everyone.' Baba Ramdev expressed his delight at the passage of the Women's Reservation Bill in the Rajya Sabha saying that since women were less corrupt than men, their presence in the political sphere would change the country at large. Also, he supports not just 33 per cent, but 50 per cent reservation for women.

The seer is vehemently against dowry system and female foeticide. According to him, mothers alone are responsible for the dowry carnage being played out across the country. He is also a strong advocator of breastfeeding since it guarantees the prevention of malnutrition and also reduces the chances of breast cancer and of second pregnancy till the mother is breastfeeding her first child. In this way, breastfeeding also helps in controlling the growing population.

Reforming Education

Highly disillusioned with the present inefficient and decadent education system, Ramdev advocates bringing back the traditional Indian *gurukul* system of value-based education. According to him, the assets and property, which children inherit from the family is not important, but the values they gather are important. He wants yoga to be a part of school education and insists it should begin from primary school level so that every child feels that he or she belongs not only to the family, but also to the society and the entire nation at large. This will encourage children to become enlightened and responsible citizens. According to the seer, the recent emphasis on introducing sex education in schools is highly deplorable as sex is a natural process; he points out that no other creature in the world goes to school for sex education! Neither morality can improve with imparting sex education in schools, nor can AIDS be prevented by talking freely about sex and by using condoms. According to the seer, English being the medium of instruction has rendered the majority of children in the country unable to study science, engineering, medicine and management. No other civilized nation of the world educates their citizens in a foreign language. Unfortunately, the 5 per cent English-educated people of our nation consider the rest 95 per cent people to be illiterate fools and harbour the view that only their children can study to become doctors, engineer, scientists or officers in Indian administrative and police services.

Rising above Casteism and Reversing Reservation Policies

According to Ramdev, casteism is yet another curse that has been playing havoc with the country's destiny. It is the most deplorable and unattainable basis for building a healthy and humane society. He is also one of most ardent critics of the government's reservation policy. He says, 'Beggars have no choice and self-respect. No Indian need be a beggar and keep begging for reservations. It would lead to worst kind of casteism and cannot help a nation grow. The recent problem in Rajasthan with the Gujjar community is an example of caste conflict.'

Containing Economic Disparities and Growing Social Disquiet

Ramdev is vehement about the stark economic disparities that characterize today's India. The daily income of about 25 crore of people is a mere Rs. 5; at the other extreme, an estimated 25 people in the same country have a daily earning of five crore rupees! The primary reason, according to Ramdev, is that the economic policies are feudal and short-sighted, and not truly capitalistic with a human face, as in some developed countries. The sage proclaims, 'The primary goal my crusade is *anto-udhaya*, the emancipation of the poorest, the last main in society, who is the worst victim of mind boggling poverty, hunger, apathy and whose rights have been swallowed by the corrupt system.' For the pain and deep concern he feels about this man, he prefers to live like him, takes little food, sleeps on the floor and has no personal assets worth the name.

Fighting Corruption – The Ill of all Ills

In his discourses, Ramdev echoes the common citizen's utter dismay at the decaying political culture that has taken roots in the country. He laments, 'All that we can see is political uncleanliness. Politics has become a business. We have gained freedom from foreign slavery but even in free India, we see high levels of exploitation, injustice, torture and corruption going on in the name of governance, and there is an environment of insecurity and disbelief in the entire country. It cuts across party lines. India is the only country where a peon (office messenger) is punished for a crime and forced out of job, while murderers and criminals with police records are allowed to become legislators or MPs.' In the present time, he says, the country is so terrorized by the misdeeds of corrupt rulers and authorities that the common man feels himself to be helpless, destitute, lonely and tired, and even while living in independent India, is desperate because of the constant fear of becoming a victim of exploitation.

Curse of Corruption and the Fall of the Nation[14]

Corruption as the main reason for unemployment: As per the seer's estimates, the total budget of the local authorities, the state governments and the central government for the development of the nation is approximately 20 lakh crore of rupees. Of this, at least 10 lakh crore get sacrificed at the altar of corruption every year. The seer further argues that if this 10 lakh crore were distributed without any bias amongst, say, 600 districts in the country, then each district would get Rs. 1,666 crore in a year. With this money as input for development of a district in a year, no one would remain unemployed in that district, and finally there would be no poverty or hunger in the country. Since everyone would be happy and sufficiently fed, hatred, robbery and other crimes in the country would be almost zero.

Reason for plight of agriculture and farmers: Corruption is leading to poor water management, resulting in floods, famines and suicides by farmers every year. The total agricultural land in India is 17.5 crore hectares, of which 10 crore hectares can be used for agricultural purposes. With proper water management, this vast area can be completely utilized and the country made self-sufficient in foodgrains and edible oils.

Reason for exploitation in place of governance: It is because of corruption that injustice is perpetuated through bribery, hawala business, exploitation by police and administration, and misuse of law. The law is used to humiliate and torture poor and honest people. Many a times, the price of honesty has to be paid with life.

Reason for unconstitutional and irresponsible conduct: When the politicians who lead the system show irresponsible behaviour and do not discharge their duties, then organizations and the people running those organizations become unconstitutional, good-for-nothing and irresponsible. As a consequence, bureaucracy becomes irresponsible and lethargic, and government schools and colleges are saddled with uncommitted teachers, and government hospitals with doctors with no philosophy of treatment. Despite the existence of a law-enforcement system, criminals and the corrupt do not get punished.

Destruction of Indian industries: When the wealth of the nation gets lost in corruption, foreign investment has to be sought for economic development. Thus, the nation's resources are given away to MNCs. In several instances, indigenous industries and factories have become victims of such conspiracies.

Reason for inflation: Because values are not properly fixed and corrupt people promote hoarding of commodities, their prices escalate arbitrarily. Ultimately, the gap between the rich and the poor gets more widened than ever.

Reason for wrong intentions and wrong policies: Because of wrong intentions, wrong policies are made so that every village has a brewery. The poor, hard-working farmers and underage children get ruined because of this addiction, and the lives of women get destroyed. Subsidy is given to slaughterhouses, which kill such beneficial animals as cows and buffaloes, and because of this, negative energy is created in the country by the cries of lakhs of innocent animals everyday. This is despite the fact that even today, in many states, land is tilled and carts are pulled by bullocks, buffaloes and camels, providing savings of millions of rupees by substituting petrol and diesel. As these animals are killed in the slaughterhouses and agriculture gets corporatized and mechanized, the productivity of small and marginal farmers suffers. Also, lakhs of rupees are spent on petrol and diesel, leading to manifold increase in pollution.

License Raj: Everything is in the hands of government officials — from a person's birth certificate to death certificate, from the registration of a vehicle to the building of a small house or a shop factory and running it, and from land registration to making of ration cards and identity cards. This results in widespread corruption at every stage of life.

Reason for extortion and robbery: Apart from corruption, entrepreneurs, who are the leaders of industrial development, are subjected to extortion by corrupt officials and politicians.

Sometimes this extortion is in the name of party donation, and sometimes in the name of elections fund. First, there is robbery in the name of elections, and once the elections are won, it is as if they have got a permit to extort.

Reason for loss of the common man's hard-earned money in stock market: Because of collaboration among the corrupt, dishonest, unconstitutional officials and businessmen, and because of the wrong policies of some irresponsible politicians as well as ineffective rules and laws, millions of hard-earned money has gone down the drainpipe of the stock market. The victims of such cheating get affected by depression, the families of some others become homeless, and some even commit suicide.

Reason for deaths of poor: The massive corruption in the medical sector flourishes on the strength of adulterated medicine, unnecessary medicine, unnecessary operations, and terrorizing in the name of treatment. The poor, thus, struggle for survival and die untimely deaths.

Reason for fatal diseases: The youth, held in the grip of addictions and sexual adventurism perpetuated by various influences, get inflicted with fatal diseases such as cancer, TB (tuberculosis) and AIDS (acquired immune deficiency syndrome), and die untimely deaths.

Bad roads, bridges and communication systems: About one lakh deaths are caused each year in road accidents. Bad roads perpetuate wastage of valuable time of the people and wastage of almost 50 per cent of their fuel as they wait it out at traffic jams. If the country has a network of good roads, there will be savings of around 2.5 lakh crore rupees in petrol and other oil expenses, and the lesser amount of fuel burnt means lesser pollution. People will also be able to avoid illnesses that are caused by pollution, including cancer, TB, allergy and asthma. *Reason for lack of sanitation:* Widespread corruption in the sanitation management system, lack of strong will to introduce waste management, and lack of law for prosecuting people who do not observe hygiene are the reasons for the extreme filthiness in the country.

Reason for lack of security in the nation: It is because of the political corruption that our politicians indulge in the cheap politics of votes. There are crores of illegal migrants in the country. Any terrorist, drug dealer or traitor can enter India and get a ration card, a voter ID card or an identity card. For a mere Rs. 50–100, transport papers are stamped to let loaded trucks pass without any checks.

Merciless exploitation of natural resources: It is the result of our corrupt system that there is misuse of these resources by government officials. The iron, coal, gold and mineral mines are knowingly handed over to mafia gangs by some corrupt people for their own selfish gains.

Reason for the insult of intellectual talent: Indians are blessed with considerable intellectual ability and talent, and they are running many important organizations in other countries. However, in our own country, intellectual talent is intentionally insulted and genuinely deserving people are not allowed to progress so that other uneducated persons claim the top rungs of government and other institutions.

What will be the national scenario in the absence of corruption? According to Ramdev, firstly, the wealth of the nation will be used for the good of the nation, and then on, the country will not be in need of foreign investment. The country will see planned growth in industrial, academic and other areas on the strength of its indigenous wealth. Exports will increase and imports will decrease so that millions of people will get absorbed in the country's own industries.

Sacralizing the Nation: Towards a Spiritual Nationalistic Resurgence

The seer points out seven national dangers: self-focus because of self-confusion; corruption; downfall of personal and national character; insensitivity; disbelief; hopelessness; and self-languor. When there is an unbalance of health, wealth and education in a society devastated with hunger, unemployment and poverty, there will be the beginning of an age of hatred, crime and communal violence that will burn the entire nation. But, as he says, there is a solution to all these national dangers – specifically, yoga and spiritual transformation. With these tools for a hands-on intervention, he envisages the bringing in of revolution in thought at personal, social and national levels, to bring in a new change in the entire setup of the country and even the world at large. According to him, 'Yoga can help in raising strong and healthy and ideologically empowered individuals who will contribute in building a prosperous and self-reliant India.'

According to Ramdev, when a person becomes self-focused with yoga, that is, when he gets linked with his consciousness and soul, he is not able to do anything that goes against his soul. Only a yogi can protect himself from the worldly attractions of wealth, position and status. Hence, the first and essential requisite in this nation-awakening mission is that each individual must be a yogi. Unless one practises yoga, self-indifference arises. And dishonesty, corruption, hatred, crime, insensitivity, idleness, unawareness, materialism and impurity are nothing but a result of this self-indifference. 'A person who is spiritual sees the nation in his body. This is because he feels that his body is made from the food, air and water of the soil of this nation. This land has given me life.'

With yoga, self-focus will replace self-confusion; honesty will replace corruption and dishonesty; sensitivity will replace insensitivity; faith will replace disbelief; hope will replace hopelessness; and the feeling of self-glory of the nation will replace self-languor. Thus, using the power of yoga for mass transformation, the seer also wants to launch virtually a second struggle for independence of the nation to build an India that the martyrs had dreamt of.

The Key Proactive Strategies

The seer has envisioned the national rejuvenation project around five key strategies.

First, he plans to reinstate the mass revolutionary zeal witnessed during the country's freedom struggle through a reassessment of the country's independence history. He believes that independence was won by the sacrifices of martyrs. If somebody says it was achieved without arms and bloodshed, it is an insult to the martyrs. He, therefore, wants to revive in the popular imagination the nationalistic stance of the country's revolutionary icons – Ram Prasad Bismil, Ashfaqulla Khan, Bhagat Singh and Hari Shivaram Rajguru, all hanged by the British rulers – and the legendary heroes of the freedom struggle, Subhash Chandra Bose and Sardar Vallabhbhai Patel, vis-à-vis what he views as the opportunistic politics of Mahatma Gandhi and the Congress Party during the pre-independence period.[15] These symbols of freedom struggle, according to him, will help in inducting a sense of pride and sacrifice among the people, particularly among the youth of the country.[16] It is ironical that he holds this view despite being a proponent of swadeshi, indigenous knowledge and natural healing, the key components of Gandhian philosophy.

The second strategy involves sensitizing a large section of people on the need of a collective moral transformation in view of the maladies of corruption, communalism, casteism and terrorism, to bring about unity and equality in society. According to the seer, 'A nation can progress in all stages if seven great qualities – knowledge of truth, devoted nature, responsibility, farsightedness, transparency, humanism and feeling of welfare – become a part of its citizens' lives. Since hypocrisy is not a good character, it is necessary to have an equal national, social and personal character.' No matter how much power, strength, position or property a corrupt, dishonest and criminal kind of person might have, one should not fear him because the soul of corrupt and dishonest people is dead and it is only to destroy them that the Lord has given birth to us in this world and country.

In Ramdev's view, the activism of all committed, wise and honest people is necessarily a prior condition. To them, he makes a powerful clarion call. 'The unwillingness of the gentlemen is more harmful for the nation when compared to the wrong deeds of ill-minded people. God has sent us on this earth to do great tasks. Therefore, you should be dedicated towards building the nation without falling into the trap of disappointment, sorrow, inferiority complex, etc. We are not individuals but represent the whole nation. Our good or bad work is related to the whole nation, not just ourselves.'

The seer's third strategy is to hand over the reins of the country to those who are transparent, humble, far-sighted and enterprising. To achieve this, he wants to create a 'leader' from among the masses. Ramdev, however, claims that he has no political ambitions, and only wishes to be an enabler of a vibrant, efficient and clean political system. He states his political thought thus: '"All party" and "no party" people with good and pure character [across] all parties are my own. That is why I am "all party". Corrupt, dishonest and criminal people from [any party] have no connection with me. That is why I am "no party".'

The fourth strategic component of Ramdev's rejuvenation project is strengthening the country's economic development by bringing back and investing Rs. 50 lakh crore–Rs. 75 lakh crore of the nation's wealth siphoned off and deposited in Swiss banks by the corrupt over the past six decades.

The seer's fifth strategy is built around Bharat Swabhiman Trust (National Pride Restoration Forum), a nationwide movement to be driven by a powerful synergic voluntarism. This mass-awareness movement envisages developing a very large vote bank of patriotic and morally strong people, and establishing accountability of governance whereby the people will direct and supervise development at all levels, enforcing use of public exchequer money in a transparent and meet-the-target-oriented manner, while launching legal action against the corrupt.

The seer, thus, seeks to transform his spiritual- and culture-specific mass-awakening doctrine into a nationwide movement to heal the nation of its ills, restore lost prestige, and bring about a radical change in all spheres of national life. His objective is to restore the status of 'world mentor' to India, in tune with the prophecy of former president of India, A. P. J. Abdul Kalam, that 'India will become world mentor again one day', though in a different context. The seer wants India to become a superpower through target-oriented swadeshi policies and actions.

For Ramdev, the successful implementation of the national regeneration project is going to decide the future of India. In its absence, he foresees anarchy and a bitter civil war perpetuated by a whole variety of vested interest groups.[17]

Agenda of Bharat Swabhiman Movement

With Bharat Swabhiman Movement as the core building block, Ramdev has set a vision of the future in terms of specific key goals.[18]

I. Healthy India

Only healthy citizens can build a prosperous, magnificent India. 'I want to build such an India in which each citizen, poor or rich, is healthy physically, in thoughts and in feelings.'

II. Clean India

For this goal, Ramdev has set Maharishi Patanjali's celebrated views on the importance of cleanliness in spiritual pursuits as the guiding principle: 'Cleanliness to be the first rule for a yogi. The universe is purified by sacrificial fires, air is purified through planting of trees, the body is purified by water, mind is purified by truth, wealth is purified by donation, wisdom is purified by knowledge, and the soul is purified by study and penance.'

When there will be spiritual awakening in the country, the character of every person and that of the nation will be pure. Pollution in food, thought, mind and behaviour will disappear so that diseases, fear, corruption, crime and anarchy will go down in the country. When the standards of cleanliness and purity are intensified, then there will be control over adulteration in food. The country will have high standards of water quality and sanitation. To make the air, food and water pollution-free, it is important to have nationwide movements.

III. Independent India through Indigenous Knowledge and Lifestyle

The country will become great by opting for indigenous industries, education, medical treatment, technology and knowledge, languages and costumes. Citizens should take a vow that they will no longer consume daily-use products made by foreign companies using zero technology, as they are detrimental to India's economic state and indigenous industries. Only then will natural resources be used for the good of the nation, and the diamond, iron, coal, gold and aluminium mines that are worth billions will not be sold for pittance.

IV. India Free from Political Corruption with 100 Per Cent Voting

To remove corruption and to ensure clean governance, voting will be made mandatory, as is the case in more than 30 countries including Australia, Italy, France and Germany. By voting right, the people will throw out corrupt politicians and bring into power honest, patriotic, brave and far-sighted people who have deep concerns for the nation.

V. Investing Accumulated Black Money on Development of Country's Poor

Billions of dollars of the corrupt deposited in Swiss banks will be brought back to the country and utilized for eradication of poverty.

VI. India Free from Hunger, Unemployment and Poverty

By developing the ten crore hectares of agriculture-capable land in the country, we will become self-sufficient in foodgrains, edible oils, fruits and vegetables, and also in the field of textiles and garments through cultivation of cotton, etc. By bringing in progress across all sectors, we will be able to bring about a dynamic rise in the national GDP and make villages self-dependent. Citizens will no longer go without food, clothes, shelter and other essential commodities, or battle electricity, water and road problems.

Each citizen will be able to live with complete self-respect, complete freedom and self-governance. When there is no corruption, everyone will get equal opportunity in terms of justice and development.

Funding Support

The funding support for the programme will be through a nationwide voluntary donation movement by reaching out to millions of people being integrated into the Bharat Swabhiman Campaign. The value of annual donation for urban people will be Rs. 21 and for rural people, Rs. 15. As a policy, no donations will be taken from the country's business houses.

Organizational Structure

The movement is being built around six main organizations: Divya Yog Mandir Trust, Patanjali Yogpeeth, Bharat Swabhiman International (an NRI organization), Patanjali Treatment Centre, Patanjali Yoga Samiti and Mahila Patanjali Yog Samiti. Fifteen local groups in each district of the country are being set-up to reach out to the masses at the grassroot level, viz. the youth, doctors, teachers, financial services, legal (comprising advocates and ex-judges), ex-servicemen, farmers, industrialists and businessmen, workers, government officers, scientists, people from arts, culture and media and senior citizens. Accordingly, 1,100 to 2,100 yoga teachers from each district, and 2,100 to 5,000 special members of Bharat Swabhiman Trust will select 5,000 to 11,000 working members who will prepare and train 5–11 lakh ordinary members of the Trust.

Bharat Swabhiman Movement: Five 100% Vows for Indians

1. We will only vote for patriotic, honest, valiant, farsighted, and skillful people. We ourselves will vote 100% and also make others vote.

2. We will unite all patriotic, sincere, aware, sensitive, intelligent and honest people together 100% and

uniting the powers of the nation will bring about a new freedom, new system and new change. We will make India the biggest superpower in the world.

3. We will 100% boycott foreign goods made with zero-Indian technology and adopt indigenous goods.

4. We will adopt nationalist thought 100% and while in our personal lives we observe Hindu, Islam, Christian, Sikh, Buddhist, Jain, etc. religious traditions, in our public lives we will live like a true Indian – a true Hindustani.

5. We will make the entire country 100% yoga-oriented and make the citizens inward-focused by making them healthy and arouse the feeling of self-pride in each one by removing the cheating, corruption, hopelessness, disbelief and self-languor arising because of self-confusion, and awaken India's sleeping self-respect by building national character.

At the launch of the Bharat Swabhiman Movement, Baba Ramdev delivered this message to the people of India:

> Come! Let us all get together to destroy the demonic forces. Let us take away the strength and property of corrupt, dishonest and criminal people, and give power to patriotic, honest and truthful people. Come! Let us all take a vow together, a pledge together, and a resolution that we will remove this stain of corruption from the forehead of Mother India. Come! We will

together arouse the lost dignity of India and build a new powerful India. We will not hand over a corrupt India to our coming generations and, instead, will present an ideal and powerful India to them — an India they can be proud of!

Some Major Actions

Clean Ganga

In 2008, Ramdev launched a major initiative called 'Clean Ganga', forcing the Indian Government to declare this scared river as a national heritage. A galaxy of spiritual leaders has also formed the Ganga Rakshan Manch to launch the Jan Jagran programme for making the river pollution-free.

Disaster Management

Ramdev's task force took an exemplary initiative in holding relief work for the victims of the Bihar floods in 2008. Not only has the Dina Mandir Trust donated a sum of Rs. 51 lakh, the trust's volunteers, under the leadership of Acharya Balkrishna, spread over the affected areas to provide food, shelter, drinking water and health care. After touring the affected areas, Ramdev spoke of the failure of both central and state governments in the management of this disaster. According to him, the government agencies, in anticipation of high-level visits by politicians, would stage a show of relief work and promptly vanish after the bigwigs leave the scene. Ramdev, in response to the mismanagement of natural calamities, has announced the formation of a disaster management programme under which disaster relief groups will be formed in various parts of the country. These groups will move in quick mode to the affected areas with a package of relief work.

Child Welfare

The mentor–orphan programme is yet another brainchild of Ramdev. Under this programme, he asks people to financially support destitute children being raised in orphanages in the country. Last year, this programme received massive support in Orissa when a call by Ramdev ensured that hundreds of such uncared-for children got the holding hands of their mentors.

Notes and References

1. The views of Ramdev on various aspects of his mass-awakening doctrine are taken from the following sources: Swami Ramdev, *Jeevan Darshan* (The Philosophy of Life), in Hindi, Divya Mandir Trust, Haridwar, 2008; 'After Human Body, Ramdev Plans to Clean Politics', http://www.indianexpress.com/comments/after-human-body-ramdev-plans-to-cleanse-politics/428464/; 'Ramdev Attacks Political System', http://forums.sulekha.com/forums/coffeehouse/Jai-Jai-baba-Ram-Deva-Swami-Ramdev-attacks-the-political-system-842690.htm; Swami Ramdev – interview, *Yog Sandesh*, (January) Divya Mandir Trust, Haridwar, 2006; Swami Ramdev, 'External Wisdom – I Want Change in Entire Set-up', *Yog Sandesh*, (August) Divya Mandir Trust, Haridwar, 2008; 'A Devotee Lighted the Lamp of Yoga', *Yog Sandesh*, (January) Divya Mandir Trust, Haridwar, 2006; Swami Ramdev, 'Imagine the India that Can Be', *Hindustan Times*, 9 October 2007;

'Golden Words of Swami Ramdev', *Yog Sandesh*, (January) Divya Mandir Trust, Haridwar, 2006; Swami Ramdev, 'There Is No Proof Required for Proved', *Yog Sandesh*, (August) Divya Yog Mandir Trust, Haridwar, 2008; Swami Ramdev, 'Self-reliance through Patriotism', *Yog Sandesh*, (January) Divya Mandir Trust, Haridwar, 2006; Swami Ramdev, 'External Wisdom – Yoga Can Build a Strong India', *Yog Sandesh*, (September) Divya Yog Mandir Trust, Haridwar, 2008; Interview for British Broadcasting Corporation (BBC) by Sanjeev Shrivastava, http://yogiramdev.blogspot.com/2007/05/interview-for-bbc.html; Jaishankar Mishra Savyasachi, 'Swami Ramdev: A Real Crusader of Yoga Culture', *Yog Sandesh*, (January) Divya Yog Mandir Trust, Haridwar, 2006; Swami Ramdev, 'Follow the Path of Vedas', *Yog Sandesh*, (August) Divya Prakashan, Divya Yog Mandir Trust, Haridwar, 2008; Damayanti Datta, 'The Karma Chameleon', *India Today*, 1 October 2007, pp. 79–81.

2. The people governing the nation would be known as Chief Sevaks. In this political system, all citizens irrespective of their religious connections will work together for eradicating poverty, corruption, harassment of women, drug addiction and alcoholism. This way, an India committed to spiritual socialism will become a model nation capable of providing guidance and help to all others. See A. K. B. Nair, 'Spiritual Socialism', http://www.bhavans.info/heritage/vision36.asp; K. K. Sinha, Uma Sinha and Priyam Krishna, *Whither Socialism: Quest for a Third Path*, Serials Publication, New Delhi, 2008; S. R. Sengupta, *Spiritual Socialism: Solution to Crisis of Civilization*, Bharatiya Vidya Bhavan, Mumbai, 1999.

3. Swami Jyotirmayananda (ed.), *Vivekananda: His Gospel of Man-Making*, 5th edition, published by Swami Jyotirmayananda, Chennai, 1988.

4. Arvind Sharma, *Modern Hindu Thought*, Oxford University Press, New Delhi, 2002.

5. Swami Vivekananda, *Complete Works of Swami Vivekananda*, Volume 1, Advaita Ashrama, Mayavati, Almora, 2001.

6. Swami Vivekananda, *Man the Maker of His Destiny*, Complete Works, Volume 8, Advaita Ashrama, Mayavati, Almora, 2001; Vivienne Baumfield, 'Science and Sanskrit: Vivekananda's Views on Education', in William Radice (ed.), *Swami Vivekananda and the Modernization of Hinduism*, Oxford University Press, New Delhi, 1999.

7. Arvind Sharma, op. cit.; Glyn Richards, *A Source Book of Modern Hinduism*, Curzon Press, London, 1985; Noel Anthony Salmond, *Hindu Iconoclasts: Rammohun Roy, Dayananda Sarasvati and Nineteenth-Century Polemics against Idolatry*, Wilfrid Laurier University Press, Waterloo, Canada, 2004.

8. Ibid.

9. Ramdev laid the foundation stone of a yoga centre being built in the place of a nightclub that closed down four years ago. He lauded the efforts of Deputy Chief Minister R. R. Patil for banning dance bars. The property, which once housed Deepa Bar, was donated to Baba Ramdev's Patanjali Yogpeeth. He also suggested converting all bars in Mumbai into yoga centres.

10. For instance, the seer is highly critical of the presence of cheer girls in cricket because it is against our culture.

11. Herbert Schiller, *Communication and Cultural Domination*, International Arts and Sciences Press, New York, 1976; A. Mattelart, *Multinational Corporations and the Control of*

Cultures: The Ideological Apparatuses of Imperialism, Harvester Press, Sussex, 1979. Also see Ashok Raj, 'The Curse of Globalised Culture: The Fall of Indian Cinema Foretold', *Futures*, Volume 36, Elsevier, London, 2004.

12. Rajni Bakshi, *Bapu Kuti - Journeys in Rediscovery of Gandhi*, Penguin Books, New Delhi, 1998; Anita Kainthla, *Baba Amte: A Biography*, Viva Books, New Delhi, 2006; Shyam Pandharipandhe, 'Anna Hazare – The Keeper of the Earth and Human Conscience', http://www.jansamachar.net/display.php3?id=&num=11507&lang=English, http://www.annahazare.org/biography.html; Mark Lindley, *J. C. Kumarappa: Mahatma Gandhi's Economist*, Popular Prakashan, New Delhi, 2008; 'Dr. J. C. Kumarappa – Out of Suit, into Khadi', http://www.kigs.org/kumarappa1.htm.

13. 'Baba Ramdev Opposes Bt Brinjal', http://www.hindu.com/2010/02/09/stories/2010020951570200.htm

14. Swami Ramdev, 'Bharat Swabhiman – Aim, Philosophy and Principles', *Yog Sandesh*, (March) Divya Yog Mandir Trust, Haridwar, 2008.

15. Such a stance by the seer, however, sparked reactions of rage among Gandhi's followers, mainly activists of the Congress Party. They charged Ramdev with insulting the Father of the Nation. Youth workers of Congress burnt posters of Ramdev and shouted slogans against him.

16. The seer also holds *Vande Mataram*, the song of the revolutionaries penned by the legendary Bengali writer and poet, Bankim Chandra Chatterjee, in great reverence. According to him, *Vande Mataram* does not mean worshiping this soil; it

means dedication towards the service of mankind and praying for the progress and prosperity of the nation.

17. George Joseph, 'Yoga Has Nothing to Do with Religion – It Is Not Hinduism' – An exclusive interview of Swami Ramdev, http://inwww.rediff.com/news/2007/jul/17slide1.htm.

18. Swami Ramdev, *Jeevan Darshan* (The Philosophy of Life), in Hindi, Divya Mandir Trust, Haridwar, 2008.

Chapter 6

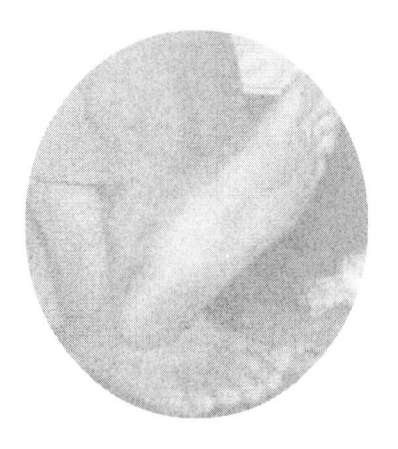

AGENDA FOR GLOBAL REJUVENATION

करें योग, रहें निरोग

The seer seeks to build a worldwide yoga and 'holistic living' movement that eventually would be extended to a global collective responsibility geared towards improving the external world.

Ramdev's mission of rejuvenating a sick, decadent society is not limited to India. After stirring the minds of millions of Indians, he has now moved to the international domain to contribute to the making of a spiritually healed world. In an interview, he was asked, how does he look at the current world? The seer's reply was like a concerned healer's prescription: 'The world [is] going through a difficult phase. Spirituality, non-violence and love will prevail, though things look difficult now. The spirituality in people has come down. The bad (*asura*) powers have taken over many people. But at the same time, things like yoga bring spirituality back to man. Eating, meeting and sitting will not change anything. *Sadhana* (practice) and more *sadhana* is needed. When discipline and devotion are lost, people become prone to evil things.'[1]

Ramdev's entry into the passionate global debate on the alternative ways of human progress underlines once again the strengths of the ideological framework for spurring mass awakening and employing this for collective resurgence to salvage the world from its spiritual, political, social and economic decline. This guru, an iconoclast per se, like several other thinkers and activists stands at the interface of the dominant, high technology-driven dehumanized ideology of development and the bubbling inspirations and ideas that desperately seek to change the world.

The seer seeks to build a worldwide yoga and 'holistic living' movement that eventually would be extended to a global collective responsibility geared towards improving the external world. In a way, he envisages the arrival of a 'new global man', a spiritually enlightened soul empowered with a transnational consciousness, devoting his newly found energies in the service of humanity, in the process negating all kinds of obscurest ideas and practices. This 'new man' is to be built on the ideals of universal brotherhood, righteousness and compassion for all living beings.

Ramdev's futuristic vision in its various current expressions, mirrors — though quite independently — the all-encompassing quest in the West and other parts of the world for a spiritual and yet politically-conscious world with the arrival of three breakthroughs in ideas and actions that have taken shape in the last 50 years or so:

(i) a search for genuine spiritual identity beyond body and mind preoccupations, and preparing the Self for using spiritual emancipation to address the large collective issues;

(ii) a universal, ecologically sustainable manifesto for human progress to save the earth through reinvention of indigenous knowledge systems; and

(iii) a cutting-edge political ideology to counter the mundane self-gratifying ideas of technology-driven modernity, the economic and social ills perpetuated by globalization, and the dominance of corporate power in world affairs.

Ramdev's vision for creating a happy, peace-loving world free of fatigue and violence is built around a set of ideological prescriptions:

(i) bringing yoga within popular consciousness both as a viable cure for ill-health and as a change agent for gaining a healthy, socially relevant worldview;
(ii) presenting a powerful critique of modern medicine and health-care system, and the ills of its haphazard commercialization;
(iii) interpreting efficacy of yoga using modern medicine's lingo and bringing this system within the ambit of modern medicine's established clinical test norms;
(iv) highlighting the secularity of yoga beyond the pale of any religion;
(v) promoting the ideals of indigenous science and ecologically empowered sustainable development;
(vi) propagating against consumerist lifestyle, global capital power and western dominance;
(vii) promoting indigenous medicine and the emerging field of herbal science in terms of re-evaluating medicinal plants for their medical efficacy and discovering a large variety of lost herb heritage;
(viii) presenting a powerful critique of the prevailing milieu of political and social decadence, as well as a political reform model to ensure socially committed and transparent governance; and
(ix) proposing a road map for building a culturally awakened, rejuvenated and economically self-reliant society.

Reaching Out to a Global Audience

Ramdev's global outreach at present is quite impressive. With his TV discourses, he has already made inroads into the heartlands of Asia, South-East Asia and Africa as well as among a host of celebrities, the professional class and non-resident Indians (NRIs) in the United States, Britain and Canada.

Ramdev received a rousing welcome during his recent visits to the United States, England, Japan and China. During his two visits to the United States, his yoga discourses were attended by thousands, including mainstream Americans, seeking personal advice or cures for ailments. Swami Ramdev and his colleague, Swami Chidananda, also taught the intricacies of yoga to around 500 actors, producers, directors, writers and models of Hollywood. Besides, he laid the foundation stone for the first international centre of Patanjali Yogpeeth and University at Houston, Texas. With a projected cost of 45 lakh dollars and an area over 100 acres, this centre will offer yogic and Ayurvedic treatment. It will offer yoga and pranayama learning courses as well as research and medical testing facilities. The centre will also have Vedic *gurukul* facilities for yoga training, a herbal garden, a *vanaprashtha* ashram (home for old people who have renounced the world), a digital Vedic library and a museum. Houston has been selected for this mission as the city is famous as a hub of medical science and education, and it is expected to facilitate setting up of linkages with a number of institutions such as NASA (National Aeronautics and Space Administration), Texas Heart Institute and St. Luke's Episcopal Hospital, and the University of Houston.[2]

Ramdev's first visit to England in 2008 saw a large number of people thronging his yoga camps held in eight cities. The largest gathering was reported from Leicester, where the camps were attended by Leicester's Lord Mayor, a large number of Britishers and aspirants from the United States, Canada, India and Africa, as well as non-resident Indians. The participants took a resolution to adopt Indian food, practise yoga and teach yoga to others.[3]

The seer also made a mark among the Japanese during his visit organized under the aegis of 'Namaste India 2007' festival held at Tokyo as the Year of Friendship between India and Japan. Prominent among those who interacted with him were members of Pasona, Japan's multibillion-dollar HR company.

In May 2008, Baba Ramdev made an impressive entry into China as well. Being under a communist regime, China does not encourage any overt show of religious fervour, with Buddhism as the exception. Now, however, Indian yoga is becoming a rage among the health-conscious Chinese, especially the younger people who want to stay in shape and take pride in their energetic lifestyles. According to Ramdev, yoga is the only spiritual alternative for the Chinese because it does not clash with their political ideology. Prior to the seer's visit, Patanjali Yogpeeth had already made inroads into the country. It has been represented several times in China by his colleague, Guru Balkrishna. A Patanjali Yogpeeth centre is also being set up in China, and will be the first such centre to be opened in that country. A team of yoga teachers will also be posted in China this year in 2010.

In June 2008, the seer chose to leave his millions of ordinary followers for a while to serve the elite when he conducted the goodwill spiritual mission, 'Yoga on Sea', to test the efficacy of his therapy in a zero-pollution atmosphere. It was a week-long yoga session on the seas off China, held for nearly a thousand yoga learners onboard the SuperStar Virgo cruise. The yoga cruise took off from Hong Kong and touched Sanya City and

Xiamen in China and Halong Bay in Vietnam. The programme was jointly organized by Patanjali Yogpeeth and Vishwa Jagriti Mission Trust, Kolkata. The seer conducted yoga classes in early mornings and held Samadhan programme in the evenings, during which he answered questions relating to various physical, mental and spiritual issues of the participants.[4]

Notes and References

1. George Joseph, 'Yoga Has Nothing to Do with Religion – It Is Not Hinduism' – An exclusive interview of Swami Ramdev, http://inwww.rediff.com/news/2007/jul/17slide1.htm.

2. 'Baba Ramdev's 20mn Yoga Centre in USA', http://www.rediff.com/news/2008/jul/30yoga.htm.

3. See 'Baba Ramdev Draws Large Crowds in Britain', 14 August 2008, http://timesofindia.indiatimes.com/articleshow/msid-3363581,prtpage-1.cms, http://news.indiainfo.com/2008/08/14/0808141041_baba_ramdev_draws_large_crowds_in_britain_london.html.

4. A package was formulated under which different rates were fixed for different class accommodations on the cruise. While the cost of executive suites accommodation was around Rs. 1.40 lakh, the junior suites, balcony, and inside accommodations came for around Rs. 1.23 lakh, Rs. 82,000 and Rs. 71,000, respectively.

Chapter 7

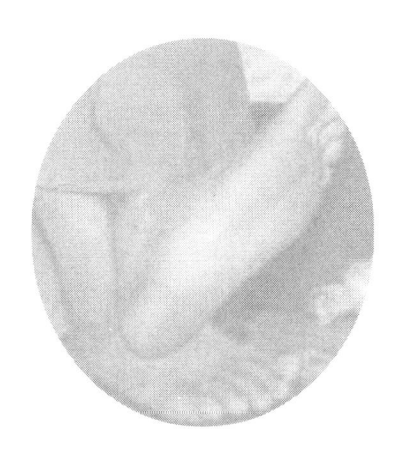

RAMDEV'S INDIGENOUS HERO'S
ASCENT AND THE FAULT LINES

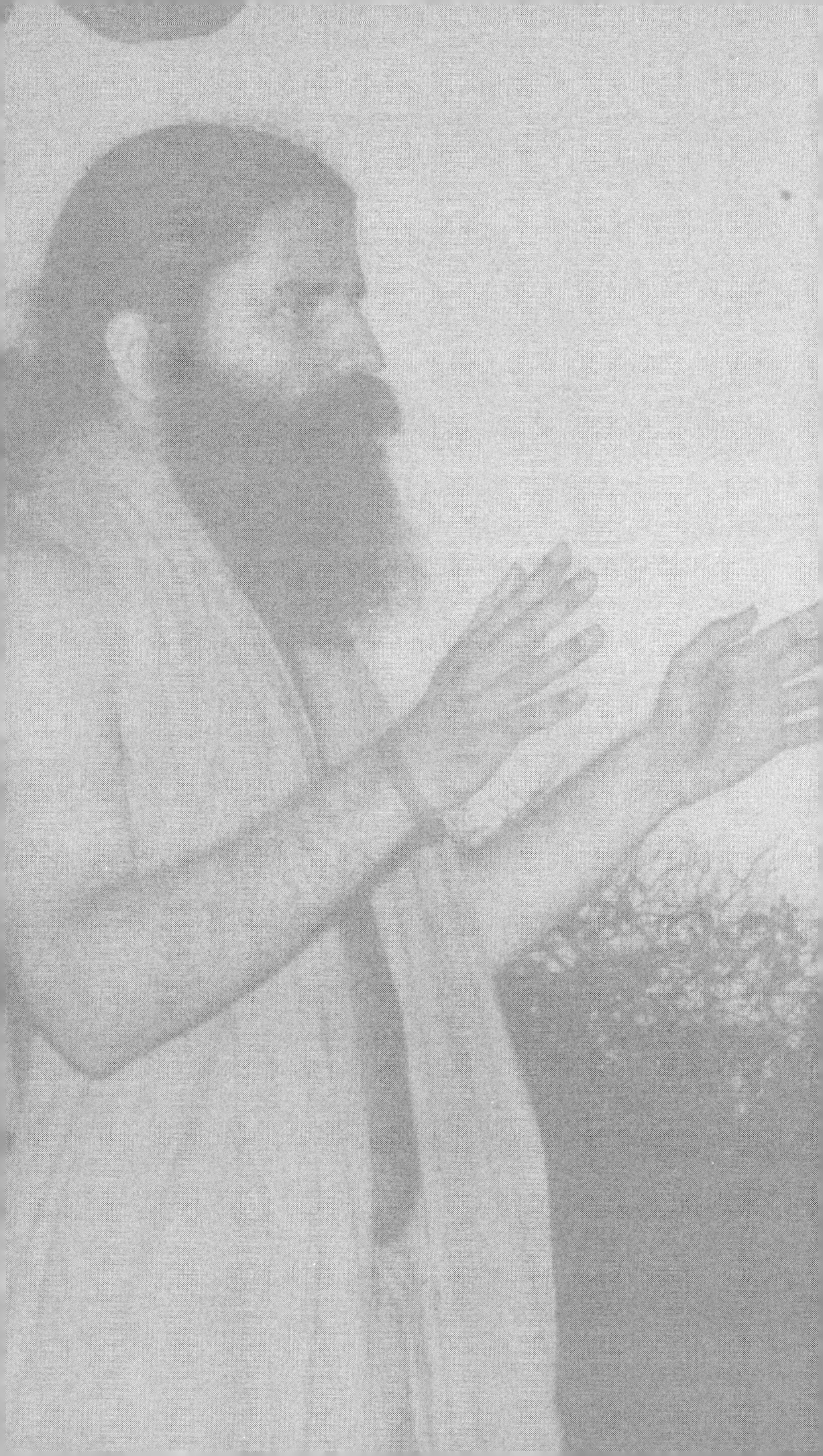

Ramdev has donned the garb of a universal teacher and, yet, in his discourses he looks as if he is addressing to each viewer individually like a personal tutor. In this age when snappy self-help books outsell classics, he has assigned for himself the role of a highly dependable healer counsellor, as he churns out – in his rapid-fire, highly assuring manner – cure after cure for almost all diseases.

The success of Ramdev's heartening image of a barefoot messiah among people endures because he evokes what he originally was — a simple-hearted ruralite with all his warmth and humbleness, and a down-to-earth instinct to create a rapport with everyone. Unlike several highly stylized, jet-set yoga gurus who largely cater to the Indian and foreign gentry, he has nurtured his 'cult' by focusing primarily on common Indian people. Much like an ordinary Indian, he lacks proficiency in English and till date he has not 'anglicized' his movement through discourses in English and other foreign languages, although they are available as translated versions. In fact, he has begun to represent the concerns of the burgeoning middle class, the small-town, non-anglicized lot, and the petty trader class, who have largely been left at the margins in the processes of free-market realization and technological modernization. Yet, he also finds favours with the traditional business class who seek to safeguard Indian culture from the all-encompassing impact of western lifestyle and culture. Several of his chief disciples are big names in the country's business and traders' fraternity. According to them, 'India needs the guidance of guru Ramdev to transform everything — be it the system, [the] society [or] the minds. Yoga cleans up minds, and only clean minds can think clean. As more and more children are getting attracted to Ramdev's yoga, we hope that it nurtures a clean and healthy leadership for tomorrow.'[1]

Ramdev, with all his charisma, also evokes the romantic notion of a guru. He brings to mind a romanticized vision of an enlightened, other-worldly figure dressed in ochre robes and followed by hordes of devotees. In the classical Indian view, a guru is an enlightened being who guides others to their own self-realization. A true 'guru' is one who removes the veil of darkness and illusion, and brings the light of wisdom through right action and wise teaching. As spiritual writer Deepak Chopra observes, Indians at large are driven by individual charisma and are not traditionally inclined towards group participation on their own. They need a central chromatic master to get turned in a collective process and consciousness.

Therefore, for people, the guru figure (like a film hero in a different context) becomes a life spectacle, full of wonder and extraordinary knowledge, a possessor of spiritual powers, the claims of which mesmerize people and make him a great seer. People are hungry of spectacles, the extraordinary, which they cannot imagine for themselves. To them, the drudgery of daily life is so ordinary and unromantic that they want to fantasize about what they are not capable of. They begin to worship the heroic. However, in contrast with other Godmen of yore, Ramdev defies any mythology about him; he is held in popular imagination as a real learned, one who is deeply rooted in reality and knows how to transfer his knowledge to practice.

Ramdev has donned the garb of a universal teacher and, yet, in his discourses he looks as if he is addressing to each viewer individually like a personal tutor. In this age when snappy self-help books outsell classics, he has assigned for himself the role of a highly dependable healer–counsellor, as he churns

Ramdev's Indigenous Hero's Ascent and the Fault Lines

out – in his rapid-fire, highly assuring manner – cure after cure for almost all diseases. His highly promising yoga package is well suited for all, irrespective of class, creed or cultural background. Furthermore, the seer is down to earth with no ambiguities in his celebrated method. Unlike several of his contemporary TV gurus, he does not engage his audience with long and winding discourses on scriptures and mythology, or bhajan singing dedicated to the deities. Focusing on the primary concern of people's health and the larger social agenda with pragmatism, his paramount concern is restoration of the self and the society. Only patriotic songs and songs for change are rendered at his gatherings.

Apart from its yoga and universal health focus, Ramdev's doctrine represents an inspiring ideological statement for a possible socio-political and economic transformation amidst the current times of desperation and hopelessness. The seer's arrival as a crusader from an unexpected field like yoga is, indeed, triggered by several factors. The state of the nation is characterized by corruption in all walks of life, by the worst kind of misgovernance, by mind-boggling and growing inequality, by a loss of direction for both individuals and society, by inter-caste and inter-community hostilities, and by an end of purposeful ideologies in the face of a market-driven society.

In such a scenario, the seer's success in building his presence in the national scene within a period of about ten years and harnessing wide acceptance of his ideas is truly spectacular. With yoga as the main vehicle and with the power of his charisma, he has prepared the grounds for leading a nationwide movement to help his countrymen heal and rediscover themselves and gain a social consciousness to serve the rapidly decaying society. In this sense, his ideology, like that of his contemporary, Swami Agnivesh, evokes an upgraded version of the celebrated reformist doctrine of the Arya Samaj. Ramdev, however, seems to have moved far ahead of the Samaj in terms of influence, mobilization and impact. As a result, he has won kudos from the common man – left far behind by the so-called virtues of globalization – for articulating the growing clash between the consumerist lifestyle of the westernized upper classes and associated wealth appropriation, and the poor multitude. His radicalism for a socio-spiritual change, therefore, is a source of great discomfort to those proponents of liberalism and modernization who carry their own hidden 'conservatism' and are least prepared to face and imbibe the proposed ideas of social change.

With his doctrine, Ramdev has also emerged as one of the few proponents of the ideology of 'spiritual socialism' in today's world, seeking its realization at the grassroots level through his national rejuvenation project to be implemented with the proactive voluntarism of his followers. In some ways, he evokes the spirit of Swami Sachidananda, the protagonist of Bankim Chandra's celebrated novel, *Anand Math*, published in 1894, who organizes his disciples to wage a war against the oppressive East India Company.

In his call for concerted action for radically transforming the nation, Ramdev stands apart from several past and contemporary spiritual masters. On several occasions, Baba Ramdev had hinted at his inclination towards joining politics when finally he made his desire public. Baba Ramdev said that the time has come for him to lead the country. Justifying his decision, he said that he was forced to take the decision because those at the helm of affairs have failed in their role. 'Political leaders have already lost their trust. Saints and gurus are apprehensive. Film stars can only act, not run the country. Industrialists don't have [time to spare] from their business. So

I am the only one left and have already started work in this direction,' he said.[2] He marked his entry into politics on 16 March 2010 in New Delhi by launching his own political party (Bharat Swabhiman), which he claimed would cleanse the political system. However, the yoga guru said that he would not contest elections or accept any political post.[3]

Swami Vivekananda, Sri Aurobindo in his later years, Paramhansa Yogananda, J. N. Krishnamurty, Sri Ramana Rishi, Sri Tirumalai Krishnamacharya, Swami Sivananda Sarswati, B. K. S. Iyengar and many others, in their preferred political aloofness, remained engaged in their religious/spiritual preoccupations, refusing to announce any political ideology that could become the basis for initiating a process of mass awakening. Vivekananda, for instance, was reported to have said, 'Meddle not with so-called social reforms, for there cannot be any reform without spiritual reform first.'[4] Interestingly, in the rest of the world, Juan José Arévalo, the president of Guatemala in the 1940s, has remained the only icon of what can be broadly termed as 'spiritual socialism'. Rejecting western-oriented liberal individualism and classical Marxism's materialist prescriptions, his ideology was directed towards the moral development of Guatemalans with the intent to liberate man psychologically.[5]

Ramdev's civilizational project is in favour of rediscovering and reinstating the Gandhian ideology in the making of a pro-people, spiritually awakened India. This is amply reflected in his staunch criticism of unwieldy consumerism, western culture and lifestyle, and modern medicine, and in his emphasis on swadeshi and indigenous knowledge. Like Mahatma Gandhi, the seer also holds the traditional business class as the honest 'trustee' of the nation's wealth, which should be spent on the development of the poor. Gandhi was a great believer in naturopathy and a staunch follower of Kene, but his views on yoga are not known.

Having ensured an imposing infrastructure and a large following of committed disciples at his disposal, the seer now has ample opportunities to consolidate his mission further to ensure its long-term sustainability. Yet, there are serious problems about his image and his doctrine, which in the long run may seriously hamper his cherished goals. Firstly, the efficacy of his healing method and its proclaimed superiority over the ministration medicine remains largely unproven. As we have already seen, he has set up an elaborate system of clinical trials in India and abroad, providing massive documentation on the healing potential of pranayama and yoga for various diseases. Yet, he continues to face much scepticism about his methods, particularly among the country's mainstream medical fraternity.[6]

The scepticism, however, is essentially due to the heavy bias of mainstream medical practitioners who are traditionally against all kinds of alternative health systems. This, perhaps, is because information is not available on the actual curing capacity of these systems, the recovery time pattern, the complete cure vis-à-vis recurrence, the short-term and long-term side effects, the rationale (including socio-cultural factors) behind the patients choosing a therapy, the initial faith and reinforced faith pattern in the system, and the affordability. Thus, in the absence of proven efficacy of alternate therapies, it has not been possible to develop health policies and practices that are based on a viable integration of various health traditions.

Given the immense popularity of Ramdev's method, the health policymakers, the medical fraternity and the international institutions should consider setting up an independent international commission to assess the efficacy of yogic cure of various diseases and its sustainability through long-term clinical trials focused on selected case studies. The Esalen Institute and contemporary researchers like Herbert Benson, Stanislav Grof, Robert Lawlor, Dean Ornish and Jon Kabat-Zinn may also consider collaborating with the seer to link their work with his pranayama- and yoga-based healing methods. Only then the efficacy of Ramdev's methods can be established in no uncertain terms and achieve universal medical recognition and appeal. Similarly, there is a need to validate the effectiveness of Divya Medicines through trials. The seer should also offer adequate space for possible failures and self-criticism. Otherwise, the massive faith the people have placed in him can easily get erased, and the very purpose of his mission will then go haywire.

Moreover, while Ramdev very strongly upholds the secular nature of yoga, beyond the pale of any single religion or community, his discourses and the overbearing use of Vedic symbolism and ideas in his presentations reveal what is rather an archetype of Hindu spiritual and cultural superiority. This is in spite of the fact that he has never uttered any livid remark about minorities and their religious beliefs, and has projected himself as an unquestionable upholder of communal tolerance and brotherhood. Much like Swami Vivekananda and Swami Dayananda, he wants to restore a sense of pride among the Hindus, presenting the ancient teachings of India in their purest form. This way, what writer Malise Ruthven says about Dayananda also holds for Ramdev: 'Dayananda's elevation of the Vedas to the sum of human knowledge, along with his myth of the Aryavartic kings, is an instance of religious fundamentalism; yet, its consequences are nationalistic, since "Hindutva secularizes Hinduism by sacralizing the nation".'[7]

That, perhaps, is the reason why the seer has not thought of including in his doctrine the virtuous ideas associated with other religions of the land – be it the brotherhood, simplicity and charity of Islam, the purity and pro-poor tenets of Christianity, the ideas of Dhamma and Sangha of Buddhism, or the ideals of self-sacrifice of Sikhism – but has been relying on the ancient Hindu religious thought and culture. He is yet to bring in the traditional knowledge systems associated with other cultures of the land. For instance, he could have easily incorporated elements of the Unani medicine system in his crusade to promote Ayurveda, as there is a lot of commonality between the two. Thus, Ramdev, perhaps due to the larger Hindu content of his discourses, has not been able to engage the minorities as equal participants in his national rejuvenation project.

From a wider perspective, as Ramdev has largely failed to overcome his dominant Vedic background, he is yet to don the robe of a truly secular mass leader and an initiator of proactive pluralism, readily acceptable by all communities. His approach, then, perpetuates the standard marginalization of minorities from his nationalistic course, as was witnessed in other Hindu spiritual movements. Ramdev needs to remember that 'pluralism is more than diversity; it implies higher active engagement with plurality. It is not given, but has to be created. It requires participation and it is more than tolerance, because of its inherent active attempt to understand each other.'[8]

However, despite all its apparent deficiencies, the success of Ramdev's secular yoga campaign has led to a path-breaking response from the Muslim community, perhaps for the first time in independent India. Recently, several members of the Muslim clergy in the country as well as in Indonesia sanctioned yoga practice for Muslims on the condition that they do not use Hindu sacred words or mantras.[9]

Baba Ramdev, on the occasion of thirtieth general session of the Islamic seminary, Jamiat Ulema-i-Hind, at Deoband in Uttar Pradesh held in November last year, told a gathering of over 10,000 Muslim clerics that Hindu-Muslim unity could transform India into one of the most powerful nations of the world. Together with Deoband's top leaders, Maulana Mahmood and N. A. Farquee, he made a call to the two communities to maintain commercial harmony and not waste their energies in hatred and violence. He also asked the Muslim brethren to adopt yoga to become mentally strong in their fight against injustice.[10] He is perhaps the first saffron-clad man to address a gathering at this topmost Muslim religious institution in the country.

At another level, Ramdev's views on certain issues like reservation of seats for women in the parliament and state legislature assemblies, and food shortage and the ability of the *yajna* (sacred fire ritual) to purify atmosphere and bring good rains and good yield reveal a rather obscure understanding of this otherwise rationalist man. He faced severe criticism for the manufacture of the medicine 'Putravati' by his Divya Pharmacy, which claimed to help women to selectively give birth to sons. According to the Pre-natal Diagnostic Techniques (Regulation and Prevention of Misuse) Act, 1994, under the Indian law, it is an offence to manufacture or publicize any medicine that discriminates against the girl child. However, the probe conducted by the Haridwar district health department failed to prove this allegation.[11]

To fight food shortage and price inflation of food commodities, the seer offers yoga as the solution. According to him, doing yoga helps kill 50 per cent of one's hunger (an idea he perhaps borrowed from Hatha-yoga-pradipika, where it was mentioned in the context of a yogi and not common people). Since the Indian middle class and upper middle class now have plenty of resources and money, they have started eating more and are getting obese. If these people eat less, the rate of inflation would come down and food would be available for the poor in the country.[12]

On the face of it, though, Ramdev, like other high-flying gurus pampered by the rich, seems to be getting trapped in a class differentiation so far as the fee structure defined for attending yoga camps is concerned – those with long purse strings get front space, while his not-so-well-off followers are pushed to the background. His recent yoga programmes designed for the gentry further speak of his growing affiliations with a high profile, neo-rich class.

Finally, it is not yet clear whether his teeming followers count him as merely a healer, a highly alluring and entertaining media performer, or, like Swami Dayananda and Swami Sahajananda, a formidable torchbearer for social reforms. His vision of inspiring change in the individual, social and national character through rigorous adoption of yoga at mass level, installing nationally committed people in the country's political institutions through electoral processes, and eradication of corruption in public life and bringing back hordes of black money from the Swiss banks presently looks rather utopian.

Ramdev's heroic dream of leading the society as a highly influential social reformer is yet to manifest into a full-fledged national movement. The struggle for reaching these goals is a long-drawn one. Unless the seer brings in all communities and public interest groups as equal partners and presents his ideology not as a mere appendage of a Vedic resurgence, but also as a powerful rendering of other virtuous traditions of the land, he will not be able to emerge as a universal mass leader.

Further, the seer's mass-engagement programmes are presently being built around his own organizational structures. He should, therefore, reach out to other like-minded individuals/groups and civil society forums working towards solving the ills afflicting the society at large. They may include Swadeshi Jagran Manch, Ramakrishna Mission, alternate medicine and naturopathy institutions, youth groups and a host of similar organizations in different parts of the country.

Despite the conflicting observations, amidst the current ideological lull in the country with no big movements to address critical issues affecting the national life, Ramdev stands in this system, all alone, challenging both the providers of mainstream health services and the powerful interest groups playing havoc with the destiny of the nation. Indeed, he has initiated among his followers a process of self-discovery geared towards collective action that can lead to the realization of his national rejuvenation project. His enigmatic persona and his forthright style certainly evoke a strange yet comforting sense of hope amid the despair, insecurity and sickness all around.

Kelly Golden, an American citizen, very aptly sums up the enigma of Ramdev in her response to a controversial article in *The Guardian*,[13] on the Internet:[14]

> I do not have a personal experience with Ramdev, and was trying not to make a judgment on his abilities or authenticity myself. Only to bring to attention that doubting and testing his healing abilities does not prove or disprove his authenticity as a true guru. My purpose was to say that regardless of his powers, it is his love

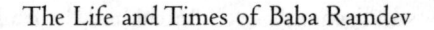

and commitment to his students that will truly authenticate his status. It was my hope to open up a discussion that would create a deeper understanding.

Notes and References

1. Swami Ramdev, 'I Want to Clean up Politics, Not Grab Power', http://www.dnaindia.com/world/report_i-want-to-clean-up-politics-not-grab-power_1168901

2. http://indiatoday.intoday.in/site/Story/87592/LATEST%20HEADLINES/Baba+Ramadev+to+float+political+party.html

3. http://ibnlive.in.com/news/ramdev-joins-politics-claims-to-cleanse-system/111595-37.html?from=tn

4. Narasingha Sil, *Swami Vivekananda: A Reassessment*, Susquehanna University Press, Selinsgrove, Pennsylvania, 1997.

5. This doctrine held that governments are capable of initiating the formation of an ideal society by allowing citizens the freedom to pursue their own opinions, property and way of life. Arévalo introduced extensive social welfare programmes, land distribution among peasants, and policies to stimulate industrial and agricultural development. The next president, Jacobo Arbenz, set out land reform proposals in a direct challenge to the US corporations that dominated the economy. Arbenz enlisted the support of peasants, students and unions to break the foreign dominance and began a series

of suits against foreign corporations, seeking unpaid taxes. In 1954, the CIA (Central Intelligence Agency) set up a small military invasion of Guatemala to depose Arbenz and install a US-supportive government.

Juan José Arévalo, http://en.wikipedia.org/wiki/Juan_Jos%C3%A9_Ar%C3%A9valo.

6. 'Ramdev Is a Quack – IMA', www.indiastandard.com/News/Social/Health/Ramdev-is-a-quack-says-IMA-chief.html; Randeep Ramesh, 'TV Swami Offers a Cure for All Ills', *The Guardian*, 14, June, 2008.

7. Malise Ruthven, *Fundamentalism: The Search for Meaning*, Oxford University Press, New York, 2004.

8. Jamal Malik and Reified Helmut (ed.), *Religious Pluralism in South Asia and Europe*, Oxford University Press, New Delhi, 2005.

9. Rhythma Kaul, 'Yoga Knows No Religion – Muslim Practitioners Find No Conflict with Islam', *Hindustan Times*, New Delhi, 10 January 2009; Renuka Narayanan, 'Yoga Is Universal, Says Ulemas', *Hindustan Times*, New Delhi, 10 January 2009.

10. 'PC Assures Muslims of Rights', *Hindustan Times*, 4 November, 2009.

11. 'Ramdev's "Putravati" Medicine under Scanner', http://www.dnaindia.com/india/report_ramdev-s-putravati-medicine-under-scanner_1094928.

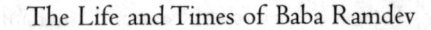

12. When the former US president, George Bush, made the controversial remark that the improved diets of the Indian and Chinese middle classes have led to a global food crisis and inflation, the seer said that the Americans are themselves very foody and the maximum number of obese people are in America, and advised them to go for yoga to curtail their consumerist tendencies. See 'Baba Ramdev Too Feels Indian Middle Class Is Overeating', *The Hindu*, 10 May 2008.

13. Randeep Ramesh, op. ct.

14. Kelly Golden, 'Baba Ramdev – Guru or Fraudster?', http://www.yogabasics.com/connect/baba-ramdev-guru-or-fraudster.html.

Glossary

acharya
acharya is a teacher of religion and spiritualism. He is held in great esteem for his knowledge of scriptures. This title is also affixed to the names of learned men.

akasa
akasa in Indian philosophy is 'aether', the omnipresent, dimensionless, incontrovertible transcendent eternal source of all energy that creates and sustains the four basic elements – fire, earth, air and water.

ananda dhvani
It is the *anahada*, the unstruck eternal sound that keeps reverberating in the *akasa* timelessly.

bandha
bandha or locking or putting together is a focused, intentional action maintained and held during pranayama by exerting pressure or force on the muscles or some other bodily or sensate processes.

brahmacarya
brahmacarya, literally meaning 'under the tutelage of Brahma', is a period of spiritual education imparted to teenage students. In this period, a student is trained in the study of scriptures and is made to practise strict celibacy.

Brahmagranthi
Brahmagranthi is the energetic knot of resistance to change, which lies in Muladhara Cakra.

Brahman
Brahman in Hindu tradition is the primordial man, the Brahma, the unchanging, infinite, immanent, and transcendent reality which is the divine manifestation of all matters – energy, time, space, being and everything within and beyond in this universe.

citta
citta is the term used to refer to the mind or one's mindset, or state of mind.

diksha
diksha is the initiation of a disciple by the guru for entering into a serious spiritual discipline and giving him mantra for spiritual practice.

Hatha-yoga-vidya
Hatha-yoga-vidya is a system of yoga which deals with the preparatory stage of physical purification of the body for meditation.

Glossary

kisan
A *kisan* (peasant) is an agricultural worker who subsists by working a small plot of ground.

kumbhaka
Kumbhaka in pranayama is the practice of retaining breath. *Recaka* is its opposite – relieving the hold on breath.

Kundalini
Kundalini in Indian yoga is a kind of corporeal energy – an unconscious, instinctive or libidinal force or *shakti*, envisioned as a sleeping serpent coiled at the base of the spine.

matha
A *matha* is a Hindu monastic establishment, which is more formal, hierarchical and rule-based than an ashram.

niscaya
niscaya means the resolve to do good to all beings and to live in accordance with the will of God driven by the realization that all beings are in actuality the body of God.

nyasa
nyasa means placing and refers to a practice in which the practitioner touches various parts of the body, and at the same time pronouncing a mantra and visualizing a divine figure. *Nyasa* is supposed to divinize the body of the worshipper.

prakriti
prakriti means 'nature', or the basic cosmic intelligence by which the universe exists and functions. It is the essential constituent

of the universe and is at the basis of all the activity of the creation. It is composed of the three *gunas* (tendencies): *sattva* (creation), *rajas* (preservation) and *tamas* (destruction).

punya
punya is merit, accumulated as a result of good deeds, acts or thoughts, which carry over to later in life or to one's next life. Such merit contributes to a person's growth towards eventual liberation.

Sankhya philosophy
Sankhya is one of the six schools of classical Indian philosophy. It is an enumerationist dualistic philosophy which regards the universe as consisting of two realities: *purusha* (consciousness) and *prakriti* (phenomenal realm of matter). *Prakriti* functions in animate and inanimate realms. *Purusha* separates out into countless *jivas* or individual units of consciousness as souls fuse into the mind and body of the animate *prakriti*. Sage Kapila is traditionally considered as the founder of this school.

shakti
Shakti, derived from the Sanskrit word '*shak*' – 'to be able', is the primordial cosmic energy and represents the dynamic forces that move through the entire universe. It is the personification of divine feminine creative power. It is responsible for creation and all changes. *Shakti* is cosmic existence as well as liberation, as attributed to its most significant form, the Kundalini Shakti.

sruti
sruti means hearing, listening, and represents the sacred texts that comprise the central canon of Hinduism. It is one of the

Glossary

sources of dharma and therefore is also influential within Hindu Law. *Sruti* is often cited as akin to the Vedas.

sunya
Sunya means emptiness or voidness, a characteristic of phenomena arising from the fact that all phenomena are impermanent and so lack substantiality and independent reality.

sunyas/sunyasi
sunyas is the order of life in which a person renounces the material world. He renounces all worldly thoughts and desires, spends his life in spiritual contemplation and dedicates his entire life towards spiritual emancipation. A member of the sunyas order is known as a sunyasi.

tarka
tarka, argumentation in Indian logic, deals with dialectics and polemics.

trishna
trishna literally means thirst and figuratively denotes desire or craving, and is traditionally opposite to peace of mind.

upanayana
upanayana is the sacred thread ceremony in Hinduism performed to mark the point stage at which boys begin their formal education.

usmani
usmani is the state of absolute stillness of mind, devoid of any thoughts.

Glossary

Vedanga
The Vedanga, literally meaning member of the Veda, are six auxiliary disciplines traditionally associated with the study and understanding of the Vedas: *Shiksha* (phonetics and phonology); *Kalpa* (ritual); *Vyakarana* (grammar); *Nirukta* (etymology); *Chhandas* (metre); and *Jyotisha* (astronomy for calendar issues, such as auspicious days for fire workshop).

Vidvan examination
This examination traditionally was aimed at assessing the scholarship of a student in Vedas and other scriptures through polemics and thorough recitation and interpretation of texts.

vyakarana
vyakarana represents the Sanskrit grammatical tradition, one of the six Vedanga disciplines. It includes the famous work, Astadhyayi, of Panini. It was evolved to have a strict interpretation for the Vedic texts.

Yoga
  Ashtanga: Also referred as Raja Yoga, Ashtanga Yoga is eight-limbed yoga in which a yogi must follow eight practices: *yama* (code of conduct, self-restraint); *niyama* (discipline and devotion to practice); asana (mastering of physical postures for mind-body integration); pranayama (mastering regulation of breath for mind–body integration); *pratyahara* (withdrawal of the senses of perception from their objects and material world); *dharana* (concentration of mind on an object/idea); *dhayana* (meditation); and samadhi (reaching the blissful state).

Glossary

Ashtanga Vinvasa: Ashtanga Vinyasa Yoga is the eight-limbed yoga, a specific yoga practice.

Bhakti: The central tenet of Bhakti Yoga is a complete passionate submission to the Divine Being along with the practice of love and devotion, which finally leads to one's libration.

Hatha: Hatha Yoga, as enshrined in the Hatha-yoga-pradipika, is the preparatory stage of physical purification of the body for going into higher stages of meditation.

Jnana: Jnana Yoga or yoga path of knowledge as laid in the Bhagavad Gita, is one of the types of yoga which gives primary importance to the knowledge of the absolute, *kshetra-jna* (the knower of the body, i.e., the soul) and *kshetra* (the field of activity, i.e., the body), and further elaborated by the Advaita philosopher, Adi Shankara.

Karma: Rooted in the philosophy of the Bhagavad Gita, Karma Yoga, in sharp contrast with Bhakti Yoga, proposes a pragmatic approach to human salvation. It demands an adherence to worldly duties but a complete detachment from one's actions and submitting his will to the larger divine purpose.

Kundalini: The Kundalini Yoga makes the awakening and rising of the kundalini power as the ultimate goal of a seeker.

Laya: Laya Yoga is the yoga of absorption in which the lower nature of mind is absorbed by the higher spiritual forces. It is based on focusing the mind in specific ways on the *cakras*, and inducing kundalini energy to arise.

Mantra: Mantra Yoga is focused on bringing the wandering mind in tandem with repetition of a mantra (words or sounds). As the mind flows with a single thought, it attains the state of samadhi.

Nishkamya Karma: Nishkamya Karma Yoga is the central tenet of Karma Yoga whereby the practitioner enters the yogic state without any expectation of a final goal. He just walks on the yogic path to final salvation.

Raja: Raja Yoga aims at physically training the body using asanas and pranayama for cultivation of the mind through meditation practices in order to further one's acquaintance with reality and finally achieve liberation. It was first described by Patanjali, and is part of the Sankhya tradition.

yoga-nidra

yoga-nidra or yogic sleep is a yoga practice to prepare a *sadhaka* spiritually, mentally and physically prior to seeking sublime levels and awareness through meditation. It is different from trance, sleep or dream state.

yoga-shala

The traditional yoga school set up by a yoga master to impart yoga education to disciples.

Index

Abhinivesa (instinctive clinging towards life), 28–29
Abhyasa (practice), 21
Absolute Truth, 24, 25, 27, 42
Acharya, 219
Adharas, 35
Adinath, 23
Advaita (non-duality), 41
Agama (Sacred Scripture, the Vedas), 28
Agriculture, 165
AIDS, 15
Ajna (between eyebrows), 36
Ajna-cakra, 94
Akasa, 219
Akasa (Brahman), 42
Alabdhabhumikatua (non-acquisition of the object of Samadhi), 28
Alasya (laziness), 27
Alcohol addiction, 140
All India Kisan Sabha, 60
Amanaska (mindless), 41
Amaratva (immortality), 41
Anaemia, 125
Anahata (in the heart), 36
Anahada dhvani, 219

Anavasthitatva (non-fixation of the mind on the acquired object of Samadhi), 28
Ancestor-worship, 54
Ancient wisdom, 13
Andre Van Lysbeth, 69
Angame-jayatva (shaking of limbs), 28
Animal sacrifice, 54
Animal welfare, 165–167
Ankit, 11
Anulom-vilom, 93, 94, 97, 109, 122
Anumana (inference), 28
Arthritis, 127, 137
Arya Samaj, 54–55, 82, 103
Asamprajnata, 27
Asanas, 35, 39
Ashtanga Yoga, 25, 29, 30, 32, 64, 68, 69, 70, 224
Asmita (egotism), 28
Asthma, 138
Asuddhamaya (principles of defilement), 43
Aurobindo, Sri, 14, 16, 53
Autonomic factors, 135
Avidya (nescience), 28
Avirati (hankering for objects of sense), 27–28

Index

Ayurveda, 24, 63, 84, 105, 106, 107, 109–110, 117, 120, 141, 158, 212

Baba, Meher, 14
Babaji, Mahavatar, 61
Bad roads, 173
Bahaya, 93, 95
Baldev, Acharya, 82
Balkrishna, Acharya, 83
Bandha, 219
Bandhas (see under Mudras)
Bang Viplav Dal, 83
Bhadrasana, 39
Bharat Swabhiman Movement
    agenda of, 179–184
    five vows for Indians by, 182–183
Bharatharis, 34
Bhartuhari, Raja, 34
Bhastrika, 93, 94, 109
Bhoja, Raja, 24
Bhrantidarsana (false knowledge), 28
Bhrumadhya (in between eyebrows), 35
Bindu (Siva), 36
Biswas, Professor Pradeep, 11
Black money, 181
Blood circulation system, 124–125
Blood pressure, 125, 135, 137
Body, 30, 35, 36
Brahmacarya, 220
Brahmagranthi, 220
Brahmakalp Dispensary, 107
Brahman, 220
Brahmananda (final bliss), 36
Brahmanism, 32
Brahmarandhra (top of head), 35
Buddha, Gautam, 33, 55

Cakrapani, 24
Cakras, six principles of, 35–36
Campaigns
    ecological and anti-materialistic, 13
Cancer, 15, 128
Caraka-samhita, 24
Caste system, 55
Casteism, 168
Chidananda, Swami, 66
Child marriage, 55
Child welfare, 185
Chinmaya Mission, 66
Citta (consciousness), 31, 220
Citta-viksepa (distraction of mind), 27
Citta-vritti-nirodha (suppression of mental functions), 26, 30
Citta-vrittis (thought processes), 28
Clean Ganga, 184
Clinical trials studies, 121–143
Communication system, 173–174
Cultural subjugation, countering media-triggered, 159

Darsanas (Indian philosophies), six, 62
Death, fear of, 29
Desabandha, 30
Dev, Swami Kripalu (Yati Kishore Chand), 83–84
Dev, Swami Shankar, 83–84
Devi, Indra, 62, 64
Dhanus (four cubits), 38
Dhanusasana, 39
Dharamveer, Acharya, 82
Dharana (deep devotion), 29, 30
Dharma, rising above organized religion to, 155–156

Index

Dharmamegha, 31
Dharmanathi, 32
Dhyana (meditation on an object), 29
Diabetes, 126, 137
Diksha, 220
Disaster management, 184
Diseases, cure for, 15
Divine Life Society, 65–66
Divine spectacle, 28
Divya Yog Mandir Trust, 105–106
Divya Yogpeeth, 131, 140
Dukha (suffering), 28
Dvesa (hatred), 28

Education, reforming, 167–168
Elders, respect towards, 139
Emotions, 29
Endocrine glands and related diseases, 125–126
Enlightenment, 101–103
Environment, 165
Evidence (*pramana*), 100
Extortion and robbery, 172

Farquee, N. A., 213
Fast food, 140
Ghantika (soft palate), 35
Gomukhasana, 39
Gopichand, 33, 34
Gorakhnath, Guru, 32–36
Gorakhnathis, 32
Goraksasana, 39
Goraksa-Sataka, 32, 34–36, 87
Gurukul Network, 108
Gurukul Kangdi University, 84

Happiness, 139

Hatha Yoga, 32, 34, 36, 37, 39, 43, 44, 66, 69, 85, 86, 87, 104, 214, 220, 225
Hatha-yoga-pradipika
 four chapters of, 37
 Swami Swatamrama on virtues of, 36–44
Hatha-yoga-vidya, 220
Health movement, 14
Heart disease, 138
Heart rate, 134–135
Hinduism, 55, 56
Hostility (*viparya*), 100
Hrdaya (heart), 35
Human faculties, 29
Hunger, 181

Idol worship, 54
Indian philosophy, 23–24
Indriyajaya (control of the senses), 30
Inference (*anumana*), 45
Inflation, 172
Intellect (*vijnanamaya kosha*), 27
Intellectual talent, insult of, 174
Inter-community tolerance, 158–159
Isvara (super consciousness), 27
Iyengar, B. K. S., 14, 53, 62, 64, 70–72, 104

Jalandhara, 26
Jalandhara-bandha, 40–41, 95, 96, 97
Jihavamula (root of tongue), 35
Jivaiman (individual soul), 42
Jivanmukti (liberation when alive), 31, 36, 41
Jnana-cautisa, 33

Index

Jnana-pradipika, 33
Jnana-sagara, 33
Joisa, K. Pattabhai, 14, 53, 62, 68–70, 104
Jyotirmayananda, Swami, 66

Kaivalya (state of absolute detachment), 31, 42
Kaivalya Pada, 25, 31
Kantha (throat), 35
Kapalbhaati, 93, 109, 122
Kapha (phlegm), 89
Kapoor, Rakesh, 11
Karma, practice of, 29
Karma-vipaka (fruit of action), 27
Kartikeya, Charu, 11
Karuna (compassion), 28
Kashyap, Ravi, 11
Kashyap, Shradha, 11
Kaushal, 9
Kayasampat (wealth of the body), 30
Khattar, Raghav, 10
Khecari, 40
    mudra, 41
Khetrival, Ganesh, 10
Kidney diseases, 126–27, 138
Kisan, 221
Klesha (source of suffering), 26
    five, 28–29
Klista (painful), 26
Knowledge, traditional, 13
Kripalu Bagh Ashram, 83
Krishnakumar, Vaidya, 63
Krishnamacharya, Sri Tirumalai, 53, 62–65
Krishnamacharya, T., 68
Krishnamurty, J. N., 14, 53
Kriya yoga, 67

Kriyas, 34
Kukkutasana, 39
Kulvalayananda, Swami, 53, 66–67, 104
Kumar, Girish, 11
Kumar, Ramajhum, 11
Kumbhaka, 221
Kundalini, 35, 36, 39, 40, 42, 70, 86, 221
Kurmasana, 39

Lalata (forehead), 35
Laya (absorption), 41, 42
Laya Yoga, 37, 225
Licence Raj, 172
Life
    deterioration in quality of, 13
    yogic way of, 14
Life force, 29, 35, 40, 43, 87, 91
Lifestyle, 15, 85, 88, 91, 110, 111, 127, 131, 138, 140, 156, 157, 165, 180, 197, 199, 205, 208, 209
Liver diseases, 138
Liver function, 127

Mahabandha, 40
Mahabhasya, 23
Mahamudra, 36, 40
Mahashaya, Lahiri, 14, 53, 61–62
Mahavedha, 40
Mahendru, Aruna, 10
Mahmood, Maulana, 213
Maitri (friendliness), 28
Malaviya, Madan Mohan, 84
Mandapa (hall in front), 38
Manipuraka (in the navel region), 36
Manju, 11
Manojavitva (speed of mind), 30

Index

Master Yoga trainers, village level, 108
Materiality (*annamaya kosha*), 27
Matha, 221
Matsyendra, 39
Matsyendranath, Guru, 32
Maynamati-govinda, 33
Mayurasana, 39
Medhra (penis), 35
Medical fraternity, scepticism of the rejectionist, 141–143
Medical sector, 119–120
Medicinal Plants Research Programme, 107–108
Medicine, ancient Indian system of, 24
Meditation (abstract), 25
Meenanath, Guru, 34
Memory (*smiriti*), 100, 139
Mental distractions, 26
Mental stress, 138
Metabolic syndrome, 136
Mind, 9, 13, 15, 24, 25, 26, 27, 28, 29, 30, 34, 36, 37, 39, 40–44, 45, 68, 69, 82, 83, 85, 86, 87, 89–92, 94–95, 97, 100, 101, 105, 106, 119, 153, 165, 169, 179, 180, 195, 196, 205, 206, 220, 222, 223, 224, 225, 226
Mohan, A. G., 62
Motor tasks, 135
Movements
  global spiritual-consciousness, 13
  ideological and spiritual, 13
  part reformist, 17
Mudita (joy at others' happiness), 28
Mudras and bandhas, various, 40
Mudras, 34, 36, 37, 39, 40
Mukta-asana, 23

Muktananda, Acharya, 83
Mula (anus), 35, 36
Mulabandha, 40, 41, 95, 96, 97
Muladhara (at the base of spinal cord), 35
Muladhara cakra (spine), 40
Multinational companies, 140, 158
Multinational products, 140
Murshid, 33
Mutual love, 139

Nabhas, 36
Nabhi (navel), 35
Nada, devotion to, 43
Nadis (arteries), prominent/principle, 35
Nadi-vigyan, 87
Nasagra (nose tip), 35
Natha (the master), 32
Natha cult, 33
Natha Samprodaya, 33, 33, 44
Nathni (female follower), 32
National security, 174
Nationwide Yoga Movement, 108–111
Neighbourhood sport club model, 32
Neo-colonialism, liberation from 156–158
Niranjana (devoid of impurities), 41
Niranjanananda, Swami, 14
Nirbija Samadhi (*anandamaya kosha*), 27
Nirlamba (supportless), 41
Niscaya, 221
Nishkamya karma yoga, 65
Nityananda, Bhagwan, 14, 53
Niyama (observance of ethical rules), 29

Index

Nur-Kandila, 33
Nyasa, 221
Nyaya, 63–64

Obesity, 126
Organised religion, 155
Orthodox Yoga Schools, 97–98

Padangustha (big toe), 35
Padmasana, 39, 95
Panini, 23
Parakala matha, 62-63
Parampada (Supreme State), 41
Pascimatana, 39
Patanjali Yog University, 105–108, 129, 182, 187, 198, 199, 200
Patanjali Yoga Samity, 182
Patanjali Yogpeeth, 106-107
Patanjali, Maharishi, 23–32, 36, 44, 63, 69, 71, 85, 87, 95, 105, 106, 165, 179
Patel, V. J., 84
Pegu, Padma, 10
Physicality (*pranamaya kosha*), 27
Pilgrimage, 54, 88–97
Pitta (fire-heat), 89
Poorna yoga, 151
Positive attitude, 138
Poverty, 181
Pracchardana (emitting the inner wind through the nostrils), 28
Prakash, Surendra, 11
Prakriti, 221
Pramada (absence of thought), 27
Pramanas (means of valid knowledge), 28, 44
Prana, 36, 40, 42, 69, 87, 88, 90, 97
Pranayama (breathing exercise), 14, 15, 28, 34–37, 39, 43, 63, 64, 71, 79, 87, 88, 91-95, 109, 111–112, 121–124, 128, 131–133, 136–143, 198, 210
    as a cure for diseases, 15
    benefits of, 92-93
    Chandra Bhedia Pranayama, 96
    Karna Rogantak Pranayama, 96
    Nadi Shodhan, 97
    Package, 93–94
    Pranav, 93, 95
    regulating the, 91
    Shitali, 97
    Sitkari, 97
    supplementary, 96–97
    the science of, 88–97
    Ujjayi, 96, 122
    various types of, 93–97
Prathamakalpika, 44
Pratyahara (withdrawal of the senses), 29, 224
Pratyaksa (perception), 28
Pravasa (out-breathing), 28
Priestcraft, 54
Psychology (manomaya kosha), 27
Punya, 222

Raga (attachment), 28
Raj, Pallav, 11
Raja yoga, 29, 37, 41, 43, 65, 224
Raja, Ali, 33
Rajas (Kundalini), 36
Rajoguna (body condition related to consumeristic and egostic lifestyle), 88
Ramakrishna Mission, 58
Ramaswami, Srivatsa, 62
Ramdev, Baba, 9, 13–16, 53–54, 79, 81–88, 93, 96–98, 100–106, 108–111, 119–121, 141–143,

Index

149–150, 152–153, 155–160, 162, 165–165, 167–169, 175, 177–179, 183-185, 195–199, 203, 205–215
agenda for global rejuvenation by, 191–200
appearance of, 15
as a new ideologue of global spiritual-consciousness moment, 13, 16
beginning of spiritual career of, 82–84
Bharat Swabhiman Movement by, 179–184
birth of, 81
charisma as an ordinary common Indian man, of, 205–215
childhood of, 81–82
early life of, 81
education of, 81
establishing medical efficacy of yoga by, 119–143
global audience and, 198–200
holistic doctrine of, 16
institutional legacy and infrastructure set up by, 105–111
mass following of, 14
mass health movement by, 14
mass-awakening doctrine of, 149–185
nationwide yoga movement by, 108–111
on casteism and reservation policies, 168–169
on economic disparities and social disquiet, 169
on education reforms, 167
on empowering women, 167
on environment, agriculture and animal welfare, 165–166
on fighting corruption, 169–175
on Hatha-Yoga, 86
on Hindu-Muslim unity, 213
on individual's emancipation through yoga, 98–101
on pranayama, 87–97
on social role of enlightenment, 101–103
package of pranayama given by, 15
personal values and lifestyle of, 111–112
popularity of, 15
predecessors of, 53–73
some major actions by, 184–85
starting mission to spread yoga by, 84
two distinct ideological alternatives given by, 14
two-pronged strategy for health by, 15
use of media technology by, 15
views on rationality by, 152–153
yoga camps by, 84
yoga discourses by, 14
yoga doctrine offered by, 85–88, 93
Ras, Madhu, 11
Rational mindsets, cultivating, 152–155
Religious cults, 32
Respiratory system and related diseases, 124
Rishi, Sri Raman, 14, 53, 209
Ritambhara prajna (the true wisdom), 27
Roe, Thomas, 157
Roy, Aeshna, 10

Index

Rtambhara-prajna (truth-bearing insight), 45

Sadhana Pada, 25, 28–29
Safi, Muhammad, 33
Sahaja (unforced intuitive natural state), 41
Sahajanand Saraswati, Swami, 16, 53, 59–61, 103
Sakhis (rhymes), 33
Sakticalana, 40
Salvation, 58, 99–103, 152, 225, 226
Samadhi Pada, 25, 26–28
Samadhi, 21, 25, 26, 27, 28, 30, 31, 40, 41, 43, 44, 71, 86, 224, 226
Sambhavi Mudra, 40, 43
Samprajnata (state of bliss), 27
Samsaya (doubt), 27, 31
Samyama (the ultimate perfection), 30
Sankalp, 11
Sankhya philosophy, 23, 24, 222
Sarasvati, Dayananda Swami, 14, 53, 54–57, 82
Sarasvati, Swami Sivananda, 14, 53, 65–66
Saraswati, Swami Satyananda, 14, 53, 72–73
Saraswati, Swami Viswananda, 65
Sarva-jnatrtva (omniscience), 30
Satchidananda, Swami, 66
Satchinanda Yoga Mission, 66
Satya-jnana-pradipa, 33
Satyartha Prakash (Light on Truth), 57
Savasana, 39
Self (*atman*), 24, 25, 29, 42

Shad-darsanas (classical system of Indian philosophy), 29
Shakti, 222
Shankar, Sri Sri Ravi, 14, 16
Sharma, S. K., 11
Shraddhananda, Swami, 84
Siddhasana, 39, 95
Simhasana, 39
Sivananda Ashram, 65
Skin diseases, 138
Skin resistance, 134
Sleep (*nidra*), 100
Social reformers, 16
Social work, 139
Soul, 25, 31, 42, 53, 71, 99, 152, 165, 176, 177, 179, 196, 222, 225
Spiritual activism, 54
Spiritual awakening, 140
Spiritual awareness, 26
Spiritual masters, 14, 16
Spiritual nationalistic resurgence, 175–176
Spiritual state, perpetual, 151–152
Spiritual traditions, Indian, 14, 53
Spiritualism, oriental, 14
Sruti, 222
Stock-market, 173
Stomach diseases, 138
Stress hormones, psychophysical effects of, 131–134
Styana (incapability of mind), 27
Sukha, 13, 101
Sultan, Syed, 33
Sunya, 223
Sunyasunya (void, yet not void), 41
Supreme consciousness, 26
Svadhisthana (at the root of the penis), 35–36

Index

Svasa (in-breathing), 28
Svastikasana, 39
Swadeshi-Ecology, 160–165
Swami, Sri Srinivasa Brahmatontra, 62
Swaraj concept, 56
Swar-vigyan, 87
Swatamarama, Swami, 36–44

Tandon, Purshottam Das, 84
Tanvi, 11
Tarka, 223
Tattva (truth), 41
Temples, offerings made in, 55
Transpiration (*viprayay*), 100
Trishna, 223
Turya (fourth state of consciousness), 41

Uddiyana (above navel), 35, 36, 40, 41
Uddiyana Bandha, 95
Udgeeth, 93
Unemployment, 181
Untouchability, 55
Upanayana, 223
Upeksa (indifference), 28
Urdhva-danta-mula (root of upper teeth), 35
Usmani, 223
Uttanakurma-asana, 39

Vairagya (spirit of detachment), 26, 30, 45
Vajrananda, Swami, 56
Vajroli, 40–41
Vakyapadiya, 24
Vara-masya, 33
Variation (vikalpa), 100

Vata (air), 89
Vayu and Prana, 88
Vayu, 88–89
Vedanga, 224
Vedanta, 23, 24, 57, 58, 62, 63, 65, 150, 152, 153
Vedas, 28, 54, 55
Vegetarianism, 140
Vibhuti (manifestation or residue), 30
Vibhuti Pada, 25, 30
Videhamukti (liberation in a disembodied state and death), 31
Vidvan examination, 224
Vidyarthi, Ganesh Shankar, 84
Vinayak, Kirti, 11
Viparitakarani, 40, 41
Virasana, 39
Visuddha (in the throat), 36
Viveka-jnana (true understanding and knowledge), 31
Vivekananda Kendra, 59
Vivekananda, Swami, 14, 16, 53, 57–59, 102, 131, 151, 152, 153, 155, 209, 211
Volunteers, healthy, 134
Vrittis (functions), 26
Vyadhi (disease), 27
Vyakarana, 224
Vyasa, Ved, 44
Vyasa-Bhasya, the, 44–45

Wahed, 33
Winds, location and functions of, 36
Women
   discrimination against, 55
   empowering, 167
   emancipation of, 62

Index

equal rights for, 57
harrassment of, 186
reservation for, 213
yoga among, 68

Yama (restraint), 29
Yoga camps, 15, 109, 121, 122, 198, 214
Yoga, 9, 10, 14–16, 23–34, 36–40, 43–44, 53–54, 59, 61, 62, 109, 121, 122, 198, 214
   aims and forms of, 26
   and Ayurveda combine, 105
   and healing philosophy, 85–88
   as a culmination of Hindu wisdom, 24–25
   Ashtanga Vinvasa, 225
   Ashtanga, 224
   benefits of, 137–138
   beyond patents and copyrights, 104–105
   Bhakti, 225
   camps, 15, 109, 121, 122, 198, 214
   definition of, 25, 26
   factors as hindrance to, 27–28
   holistic, 13, 16, 23
   Indian, 23
   individual's emancipation through, 98–101
   Jnana, 225
   Karma, 225
   Kundalini, 225
   Laya, 225
   Mantra, 226
   medical efficacy of, 119–143
   Nishkamya Karma, 226
   psychosomatic effects of, 136–137
   reinventors of, 61–73
   secularizing, 103–104
Yoga-Dharana, 87
Yoga-kalandar, 33
Yogananda, Paramhansa, 14, 53
Yogangas (methods of achieving knowledge of the Self), 29
Yoga-nidra, 226
Yogasana (posture), 29
Yoga-shala, 226
Yoga-Sutras, 23-24, 25, 31, 44, 45, 63, 69, 71, 85, 87
Yoga-Vedanta Forest Academy, 65
Yogendra, Dr Jayadev, 68
Yogendra, Shri, 14
Yogendra, Shri, 53, 67–68
Yogis (Muslim), 33

181